Suzy Becker

ONE GOOD EGG

an illustrated memoir

BLOOMSBURY
New York | London | New Delhi | Sydney

Published by Bloomsbury USA, New York

Bloomsbury is a trademark of Bloomsbury Publishing Plc

All papers used by Bloomsbury USA are natural, recyclable products made from wood grown in well-managed forests. The manufacturing processes conform to the environmental regulations of the country of origin.

Library of Congress Cataloging-in-Publication Data

Becker, Suzy.
One good egg : a memoir / Suzy Becker.—1st U.S. ed.
p. cm.
Includes bibliographical references and index.
ISBN 978-1-60819-276-2 (alk. paper hardcover)
1. Becker, Suzy. 2. Infertility, Female—Patients—United States—Biography. 3. Mothers—United States—Biography. 4. Fertilization in vitro, Human—Popular works. I. Title.
RG135.B43 2013
618.1'780092—dc23
[B]

2012043595

First U.S. edition published by Bloomsbury in 2013
This paperback edition published in 2014

Paperback ISBN: 978-1-60819-326-4

1 3 5 7 9 10 8 6 4 2

Designed by Cia Boynton | Boynton Hue Studio

Printed and bound in the U.S.A. by Thomson-Shore, Inc. Dexter, Michigan

To three great eggs

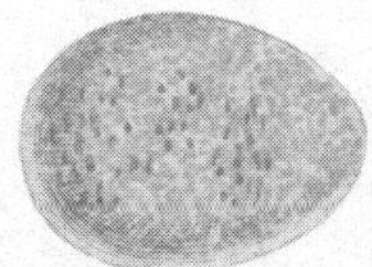

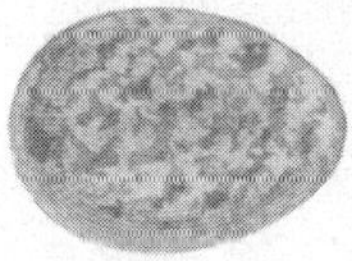

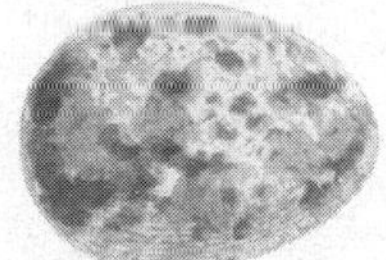

What Took Me So Long
(The Condensed Version)

It's probably not healthy wanting desperately to be something you're not, especially if it's extinct, but there were plenty of times right up through 2003 when I wished I was a Southern gastric brooding frog. No gastric brooding frog husband to find. No career to worry my shiny frog head. Life could be as simple as swallowing a batch of fertilized eggs and burping up some babies.

SOUTHERN GASTRIC BROODING FROG

The female frog swallowed her fertilized eggs, incubated them in her stomach for six to seven weeks, and then regurgitated her young. Scientists were looking into her ability to shut down her digestive system during incubation with the hope that it would lead to treatment for ulcers. But the frog became extinct in the mid-1980s.

What about treatment for FERTILITY?

For the first twenty-three years of my life, I was sure I'd have babies, at least two. Then it took me fifteen years to decide to go ahead and have just one.

From my journal
- AGE 9 -
I would like to have
4 of my own babies
+6 adopted
10

My mother got married and had her first baby in her early twenties. In the decades that followed, the average age of first-time mothers steadily rose; one third of first-time moms are now over the age of thirty. The number of single mothers and the number of women who opted not to have children also rose.

Having options is liberating, except for the parts of you that are tied up in making (and remaking) the decision.

NORTHERN BABY DECISION BROODING WOMAN

Ages 7–25	25–30	30–32	32–36	36–38	38
Baby with husband Jack, Chris, Robert, George, Tripp, Butch, Pat, Nick, Olivier	Baby with Amy and David and Paul or Steve and Gary	No baby	Baby alone???	No baby	*Baby alone!!!*

When I was thirty-eight, I finally gave up on finding true love. I had everything else I needed—the career, the home, the friends, the family, and the gumption—to go ahead and have a baby on my own.

FORGET LOVE.
I'M GOING to
HAVE a BABY!

In the end, I made my Baby Decision in a half minute on a clear cold February night in 2001 as I stood at the edge of my driveway watching my EX- partner pull out: beagle, belongings, and all.

TO DO

TO GET READY

- #1 → Appt. with ob/gyn
  - Tube test?
- Talk to Bruce
- Write to steve
- Sperm donation
- Insemination
- Clean office
  - " attic, basement
- Fix chimney
- Convert barn?
- Nursery -
  - paint
  - rug
  - dresser
  - crib
  - changing table
- New car, carseat
- Change will

with ANOTHER LOVER some day

- Hardwick Store (breakfast)
- Hotel in Newport (with saltwater pool overlooking bay)

CONTINUED

- Talk to Carol, Deb
- Fix stone wall
- Nanny - 20 hours
- House cleaner

My old gynecologist had left private practice to spend more time with her kids. I took a referral for a new ob-gyn out of the "Baby" folder I kept in the front of my filing cabinet and dialed the number.

"What is this in regard to?"

What this is in regard to would be what this is regarding which is, "Single parent pregnancy?"

"We don't do that here." She gave me the phone number for an IVF clinic and hung up.

IVF clinic?

in vi•tro fer•til•i•za•tion (IVF) *noun:* A procedure in which eggs (*ova*) from a woman's ovary are removed. They are fertilized with sperm in a laboratory dish, and then the fertilized egg (*embryo*) is returned to the woman's uterus.

I got another referral and I was connected to a nurse named Mary regarding my interest in "alternative insemination."

First question: my birth date. "That makes you . . . "

"Thirty-eight."

"Thirty-eight?" she paused. "We'll have to see whether it's even possible." Mary's tone did not ring with possibility. "You've been getting regular periods? You'll need to do Day 3 labs, Day 12 follicle studies. And the father will have to be completely tested; he is a potential liability for us. His sperm needs to be washed and frozen. This is all very expensive and your insurance won't pay; well, we do have one patient, but—you'll have to check."

"I thought the sperm works better if it's fresh."

"It does. Now, you're also going to need a dye test to make sure your tubes are clear. There's a lot to do, and like I said, it all adds up. Of course we'll try to keep the costs down; maybe if your day twelves are okay we can skip the day fourteens. Did you want to make an appointment for a consult?"

BABY at 38?!
Suzanne-
what have you been
SMOKING?

"Yes, please."

"And you said you were thirty-eight, right?"

"That's right." Not forty-eight, seventy-eight, or 138. Just plain thirty-eight.

Mary, I'm a dreamer, not a smoker.

"She can see you on March 29th."

And I want you to know, I'm not one of those OMG-I-forgot-to-have-a-baby thirty-eights. It's just that life does not always go as planned.

	– **35**	eggs per day
×	**35**	days
	– **1225**	eggs

Let's start with how I had been planning on having a career in international relations, then spring of my senior year, weeks away from earning degrees in International Relations and Economics, I discovered my favorite class at Brown.

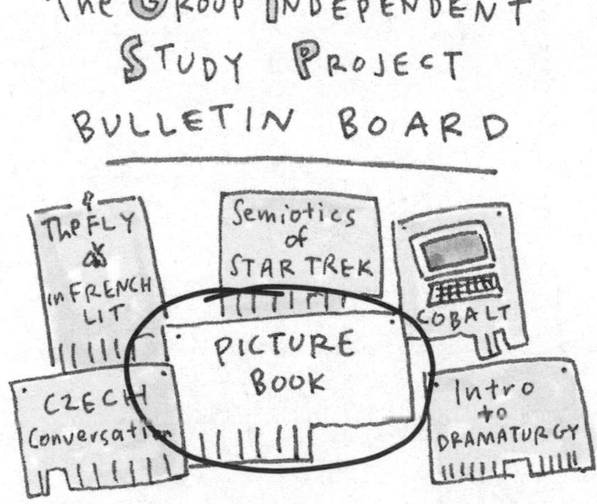

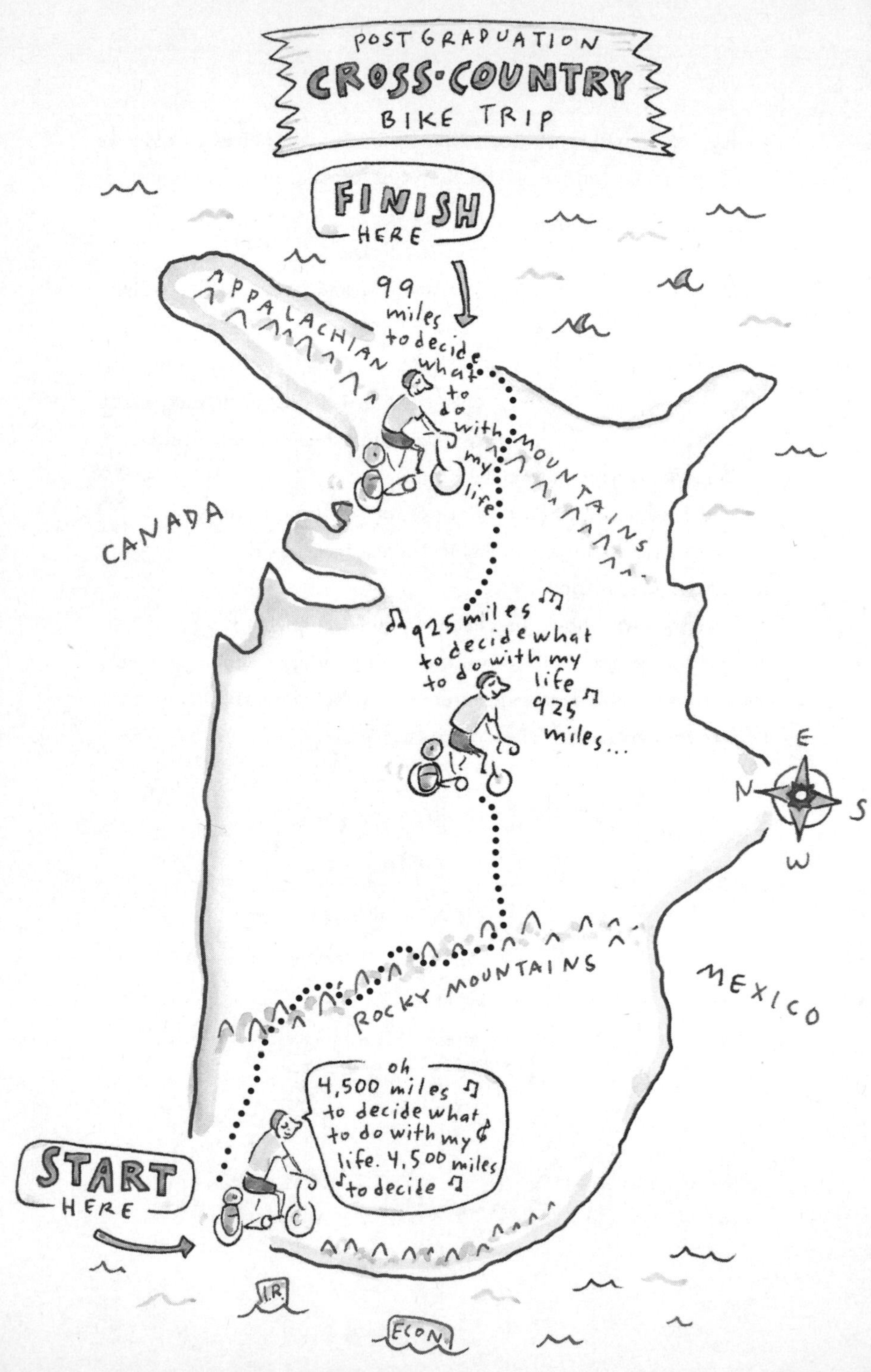
POST GRADUATION
CROSS-COUNTRY
BIKE TRIP
FINISH
HERE
99 miles to decide what to do with my life
APPALACHIAN MOUNTAINS
CANADA
925 miles to decide what to do with my life 925 miles...
E
N
S
W
ROCKY MOUNTAINS
MEXICO
oh 4,500 miles to decide what to do with my life. 4,500 miles to decide
START
HERE
I.R.
ECON.

I ended up living with my parents for a few months after the bike trip, and then I moved up to Boston, where I had a very short career as a copywriter.

> Jane will be quite an old maid soon . . . she is almost three and twenty! Lord, how ashamed I should be of not being married before three and twenty!
>
> Jane Austen
> *Pride and Prejudice*

Then I left advertising to start a greeting card company. That partnership went bad inside of six months. I mention it, Mary, because I think it is the only other big life decision I'd ever made. I had to come up with a lot of money to buy the business, or else walk away.

Actually, it wasn't the only other big life decision, but the third one didn't feel like a decision. It felt like falling in love. That winter I was living at home, I had my first romantic relationship with a woman—Amy, the leader of the cross-country bike ride. She was the other reason I moved to Boston. To put 250 miles between us, so I could make up my mind whether I wanted to be with a man or with Amy.

I dated a half dozen very nice men in Boston, but I was in love with Amy.

Wait, Mary, before you put me in a box—
say Amy was Andy, or Arnie,
Arthur,
Adam
—a lot of my story could pass for infertile-straight.

Amy and I moved in together. We found the perfect place: a carriage house with a garage (for all the greeting cards), a basement office with separate entry, and a second bedroom that could double as Amy's office *or* a nursery.

Fast-forward to age thirty. I had everything in place—the relationship, the career, the house. Then I went and fell in love with a funny folksinger who was also all but married and didn't want anything to do with kids.

Mary, some of your silences strike me as judgmental even though I know you mean to be respectful.

I dated men, I dated women. I gave up on dating. I decided to have a baby alone, and then the father's offer fell through.

At that point, I was thirty-four, the same age as my mother when she had me. People were giving up on my marriage prospects. My friends thought I was too picky and didn't mind saying so. My handyman said,

"Sue, after thirty, you start to get set in your ways. I'm not saying it's good or bad, it just gets too hard to live with someone else." I'm hearing him. I'm hearing everybody. And I'm hearing my biological clock ticking. I know I really have to make this decision.

decide · make up my mind . shit or get off the pot fish or cut bait quit dithering · dilly dallying . . . . hemming and hawing: put up or shut up · pick a plan and stick with it!

This is when I met Karen, the ex with the beagle and belongings who just left me. We're almost at the end here, Mary.

On our first date, I told Karen I wanted to have kids. She told me she had no interest in being pregnant, but her friends all said she'd make a really good dad. Well, three months later, she flip-flopped—no kids, not hers, not mine, no way, no how—only by then we were in love.

Here's the un-universal curveball part: Six months post-Karen's flip-flop, I had a grand mal seizure and I ended up being diagnosed with a mass on my brain which required brain surgery, and that unexpectedly led to some temporary loss of my abilities to speak, read, or write. I was on antiseizure medication and in speech therapy and had to back-burner my next book project. I remember stammering something to a neuropsychiatrist about being afraid I couldn't do it, meaning write the next book, and she said, so casually, "Have a baby? Let's not rule it out just yet." "Let's," you know, like maybe she and I were going to have the baby, and "yet," like . . . never mind.

By the next spring, that was last spring, I was starting to feel more like myself. One afternoon, I went back to my car to feed the meter and I found a rosebud-patterned baby dress laid out on the navy-blue hood. I don't know if you believe in Signs from the Universe, Mary, but this was my third in three months. The first was a pristine white lace baby's bonnet sitting on a post at the head of a trail I hiked during mud season. And the second: a baby bib tied to the tree at the end of my driveway. Anyway, I put the baby decision back on the table. I went to a seminar on artificial insemination.

SIGN from the UNIVERSE

I bought a basal body thermometer.

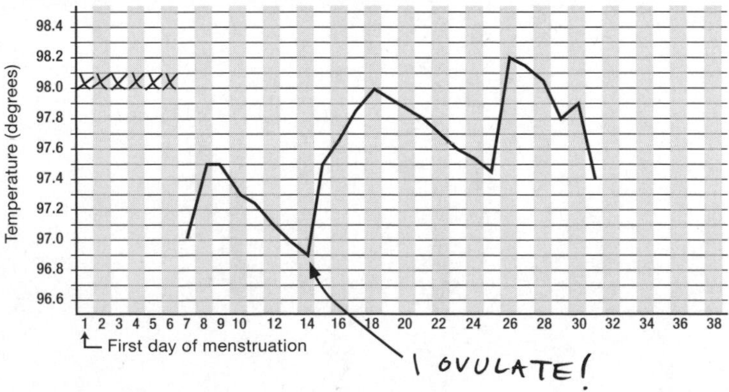

I convinced Karen to go to a support group for couples considering parenting, even though she never really was considering parenting. I was the one; I was supposed to decide so we could both get on with our lives.

It's awfully hard to pit an imaginary baby against a real live relationship, Mary. Paralyzing, in fact. But then I had an epiphany.

Wanting to have a baby had always meant not wanting to be with Karen. But when I separated the baby and Karen, when I made them into two decisions— SNIP! Do you want to be with Karen? Yes! Do you want to have a baby? Yes!

I could make them.

IMMOBILIUS STRIP

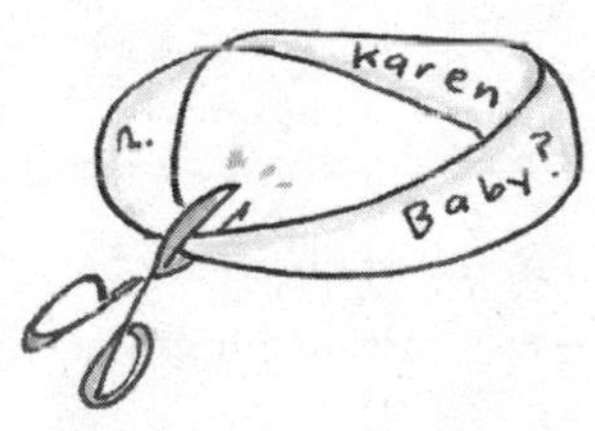

Karen mistakenly opened an old e-mail from my friend in Melbourne before I ever got to make use of my epiphany.

From: Steve
Subject: A New Channel
Date: November 17, 2000

Dear Suzy,

Thanks for your letter. This is strange-- I'm not used to typing or e-mailing anything to you. I'll keep this short; my aim is to open up a new channel. So, where to start? Baby, I guess. I can see a whole heap of practical issues, yet I have this innate trust in you. I told my friend Diane it's kind of a puzzle, not one that provokes anxiety, but one that is a bit exciting. I think you're telling me you want to be a father, she puts it to me, and I tell her, yes, I think it could be nice.

Love, Steve XOXO

Karen concluded I was trying to have a baby behind her back, packed up, and left me the night before last.

So there it is, Mary. How I got to be thirty-eight and childless.

This conversation has been so helpful, thank you. I have always wanted to have a baby.

My INNER CHEERLEADER

I'm still a little afraid, but I'm done letting my fears stand in my way. I know what you think, Mary. I really hope it's not too late. All I can do is try.

Step Two

I had the Day 12 follicle test. I went in, slightly nervous, not knowing what to expect—most likely an internal exam, possibly a blood test—and the nurse practitioner (not Mary) examined my head. I passed the test. She showed me the special hairs above my right ear, hairs I'd never noticed before, but once she pointed them out, they were very obvious. Each one had a tiny cup holding a very tiny egg. In my dream, I felt like Horton carrying around these precious eggs.

The appointment with my new gynecologist was a quickie. In and out in under ten minutes. "Suzanne, when was the last time you were seen?" *Last time I was seen . . .* "Never mind. When was your last period?" *Last period, last period*—"I'll have Ellen schedule your Day 3 labs and HSG."

"HSG?"

"A hysterosalpingogram. A test to make sure your tubes are clear." Oh, the expensive one Mary had mentioned.

"How much will that—?"

"This will all be covered under infertility. Any questions?" Wait, *are you saying I'm infertile?!* She rose, I rose, we shook hands, and Ellen escorted me to an examining room where, with the aid of a calendar, I was able to reconstruct my last period.

In the end, it didn't make a drop of difference; I needed to call on the first day of my next period and then come in for a blood test two days later. Meantime, Ellen advised me to purchase an ovulation predictor kit (OPK) and use it, following the directions on the box. I planned to save my $16 until I had my Day 3 lab results.

I called my friend Lorene with a progress report. In the weeks since I'd been single, she and I had settled into a pattern of daily breakfast calls and weekly dinners. This was a midmorning update. "Well, I wasn't going to say this while you were with Karen," she said. "But having a baby was the best thing I ever did."

Lorene and her twenty-one-year-old son, David, lived in the house where she had grown up (and her mother before her) in Hudson, the next town over.

"I'll come to the birth. Babysit. Do daycare. You can drop him off; you can give me Mister, too!"

She already took care of Mister, my flat-coat retriever, when I went away. "I'm serious. I love babies. He's all yours when he's thirteen . . ."

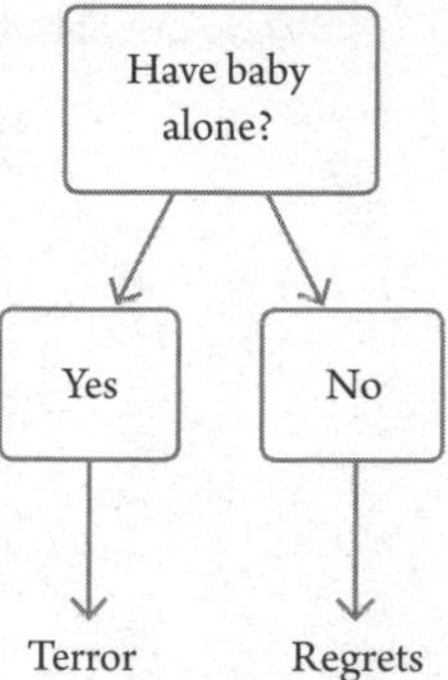

The whole time, I had been thinking I was going to have this baby *alone*. Plenty of people had offered to help, but they were well-meaning, overly busy people who weren't their own bosses, and they didn't live three miles away.

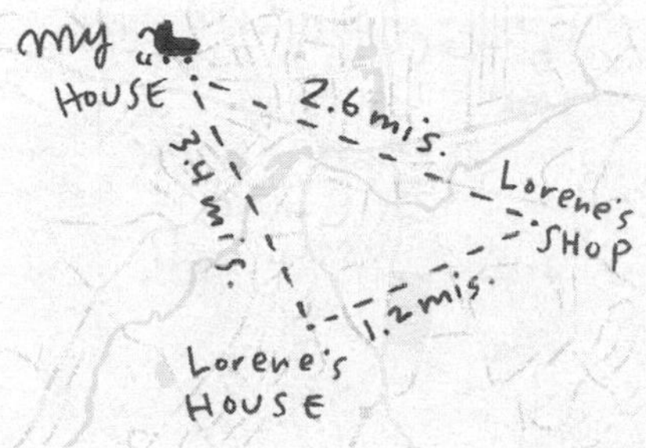

"So when are you going to tell Steve? Is that next?" Lorene asked.

"You mean *ask* Steve." I'd met Steve and Gary twelve years earlier, back when Amy and I were vacationing in Skyros, Greece. The four of us got along so well we'd joked about partnering up, marrying (this was way before same-sex marriage was legal), and having babies together. Steve and I were writers and we'd kept in touch. He'd renewed the baby offer several times; however, he could always renege, now that it was real. "I'm going to ask Bruce first."

Bruce is my best friend. We'd been spending Saturdays together for more than ten years by that time. He would make a great father, but he wasn't ready back then. Asking was a foregone rejection.

When our Saturday rolled around, we met at Café Algiers in Harvard Square. The tables were tight . . .

. . . so tight I couldn't bring myself to ask him the question.

We were in my car, more than halfway home, and I was desperately seeking a segue. Bruce was describing a friend of his: "He always asks, 'Why would you want to spend time with me?' The question makes me feel completely cornered."

"Uh, speaking of questions that make you feel cornered, would you be the father of my baby? I mean, I'm set to go ahead with Steve—it's just that when Steve and I made the plan, you were twenty-two and we were just becoming friends. I know if you were going to do this, I'd wonder, 'Why didn't he ask me, or at least have a conversation?' So that's what this is, the conversation." *Or monologue*. It was starting to rain. I went on, "I really don't want the question to torment you. I know you'll be in the baby's life either way." The wipers smeared the windshield. "I—well, you would've said yes by now," I stopped.

"It's the timing. I feel like I haven't had enough experiences or relationships."

I let him finish. I didn't say, "I know," or, "It's not the end of experiences."

"If there was anyone I wanted to do this with, it would be you. Even this afternoon, while we were sitting there, I was wondering if I could ever have this kind of love with a partner. There have been these times when, I swear, I wish I could just ask you to marry me, that it could be that uncomplicated, that there wouldn't be these missing pieces . . . "

We happened to be passing by the turnoff to Bruce's parents' road. I put my blinker on. "Let's go tell your parents we're getting married and we're going to have a baby!"

He flipped it off, laughing.

"Can I just say one thing about the timing?" I didn't wait for an answer. "It's taken me years to recognize there isn't going to be a perfect time—a time when everything's lined up, pointing in the direction of a baby. And a lot of time can go by while you're waiting. It's kind of like peak foliage . . . and now I've got to worry about my biological clock."

"That's why I don't want to say no without taking some time to think about it."

He took until the next Saturday, and then he said no, just as I expected, but it was still hard to hear. "I wish I could say yes," he said, and I hugged him. I hadn't been ready at thirty-two either.

That night, I e-mailed Steve. I waited fifteen minutes for an instant reply, then shut my computer off and went downstairs. An hour later, I went back up and turned it on again, just to check.

> **From:** Steve
> **Subject:** Ring ring
> **Date:** April 26, 2001
>
> If you think you can do it, I think we can work out the logistics.
> Call me Thursday or Friday!

Sunday morning, I woke up and called Lorene while I was still in bed. She was happy for me, but she wasn't available to celebrate. She was getting ready to go away for three weeks.

I am going to be a *single* mother.

If I'm lucky.

I Can, He Can, We Will

The receptionist at the sperm bank was initially sympathetic, generically speaking, on a par with pet-cremation or funeral-home personnel. But once she got the picture—there was no terminal illness involved, Steve had *not* been called up to war, and, in fact, we weren't even married—she went cold. "We have criteria for 'selected donors.' They must be between the ages of eighteen and thirty-eight."

"Thirty-eight?" I had lost track of Steve's age, but I knew it was older than mine.

"Six months quarantine—"

"My friend is older than thirty-eight."

A moment's silence. "A complete physical, semen analysis, and blood work, all subject to review by our doctor."

"Excuse me," I interrupted a third time. "Are you saying you don't bank sperm for people who are older than thirty-eight?" *You are a fucking STORAGE facility! No pun intended.*

She did not respond. "Ruth"—I had written her name down on the top of my page—"can you pretend like you are trying to *help* me?"

"Would you like to speak with our director?"

"I would, please. Thank you."

"He's not available. I will let him know."

Would you like a million dollars? How 'bout a pony? I was replaying the conversation for Lorene over dinner, a bon voyage dinner at my house, that night.

"Why didn't you just say he was your husband?"

"I don't know." I *did* know, but I find my own earnestness so unbecoming.

A.I.

Honesty Badge

"I don't want to bring my baby into the world with a lie. The kid is going to have to answer so many questions—a lie just complicates things."

"It *is* complicated."

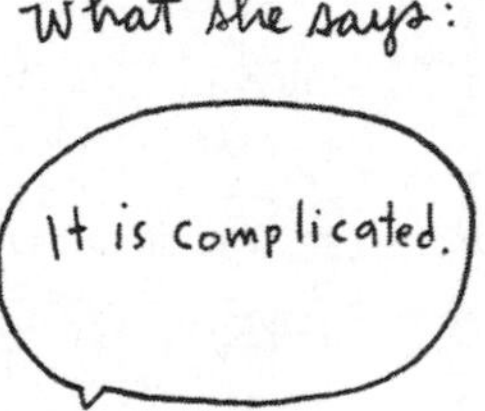

What I hear:

It's TOO complicated. You shouldn't do it. There's a reason why it's complicated. It's WRONG.

"A lot of things are . . . I don't have a simpler way." I felt like I might start to cry.

Lorene tapped my knee. "It doesn't mean you shouldn't do it. You are going to do it. And you're going to be great at it."

I was going to miss Lorene. I hugged her dog, Vita, as we watched her get into her car. Three weeks with no dinners, no morning calls.

The phone rang at six o'clock two mornings later. I'd already fed Vita and Mister and gone back to bed. I could hear church bells ringing in the background. Lorene was just calling to get my shoe size. I fell back to sleep.

Lorene was sitting on my bed. She had presents for me: little pastel-colored tissue paper party favors that became animals and a metal letter holder with animal cutouts. I hugged her and she said, "I was looking for love in your eyes. I must have masticated this." I knew she meant "fabricated."

The dream was as unsettling as it was pleasant. I couldn't be falling in love again—not with the best friend I'd made in a very long time. Besides, it was much too soon.

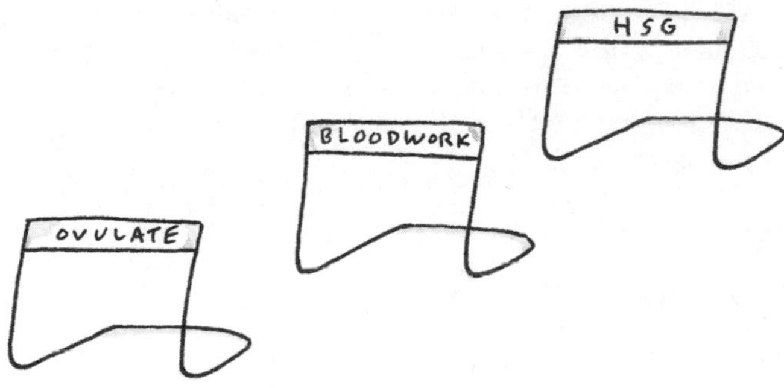

My Day 3 blood work was normal; I got the news on Day 4. My fertility was in question for less than twenty-four hours. Meanwhile, on the other side of the world, Steve waited weeks for his results.

> **From:** Steve
> **Subject:** Testing, testing
> **Date:** June 5, 2001
>
> Hi Suzy, Well, it's done. I was escorted into a white room with a coffee table and a magazine called Home Girls, offering "50 Top Titties." I was given a curiously small container, not that I was going to fill it—it's just the mechanics of getting the stuff in there. The nurse said, "Are you sure that's the whole deposit?" I've been staying up until 2 a.m. watching the French Open. Now she's got me worried. I'll let you know when I hear. Probably a week. I want Capriati to win the tittle, oops, title.
> Love, Steve

Eleven days later:

> **From:** Steve
> **Subject:** Still waiting
> **Date:** June 16, 2001
>
> My GP has a mystery illness, no one knows when she'll be back and the results must come through her. The secretary assures me the results are not in; it could take another seven days. (The lab typist is slow.) I'm half-convinced I'm not fertile. Friends tell me the sperm pool is drying up due to pollution, preservatives, and pay TV. The way I see it, if I'm fertile, that's great. Fine adventures ahead. If not, that's also okay—other adventures ahead, but I'm hoping, a bit afraid.
> Love, Steve

Another nine days later:

> Hey Suzy, Guess what—I'm fertile! All the results came up okay.
> More later, xxx, Steve

Lorene brought me shoes from Italy. And a baby board book in Italian. And my baby's first toy. I was looking into his bead eyes, imagining that baby, when Lorene said, "I shouldn't have. Here," she reached for him. "I'll keep him. I'm sorry. You're afraid I've jinxed you."

"No," the thought hadn't occurred to me. "I'm afraid." I hesitated. "I'm falling in love."

"Oh." She laughed for a few uncomfortable seconds. "Me, too. But we know better."

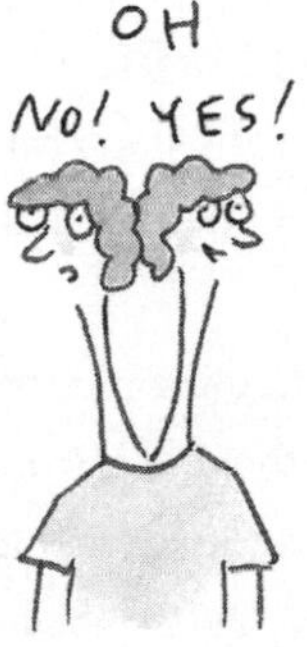

I agreed. Neither one of us was about to trade a lifelong best-friendship for another short-lived love affair.

And for a full fourteen days we didn't. Then the night before I was leaving for Milwaukee, we kissed good-bye.

SIGN from the UNIVERSE

HOROSCOPE: LIBRA ♎

When two Libras come together in a love affair, they form one of the most agreeable, romantic and well-balanced relationships around . . . Libra loves to be in love, and two together spells relationship bliss.

I would have a week on my bike, cycling through Door County (the tip of the thumb of Wisconsin) to consider, reconsider, and re-reconsider what we had done. But by the time I changed planes in Minneapolis, I was convinced I had done one of the best things in my life.

There was another sign written in the stars. We both loved the name Aurora for a girl.

Aurora

ORIGIN Latin; meaning DAWN, *Aurora Borealis, Aurora Australis* – Northern and Southern Lights named after Roman goddess of dawn. This name is popular in Italy, Norway, Switzerland.

I came up with DILLON (Steve's last name) JEAN (Lorene's last name) BECKER for a boy. Steve "quite liked the ring to it."

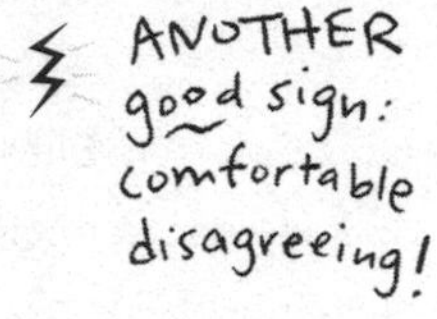

"Dildo Pecker?" Lorene nixed it. "You can't do that to a kid!"

ANOTHER good sign: comfortable disagreeing!

In the month that followed, Lorene moved in little by little. A pillow, the dog's bed, an extra cutting board, her favorite bowls, the popcorn popper. Her music would be drifting out of windows I had never opened when I came home from my morning bike rides.

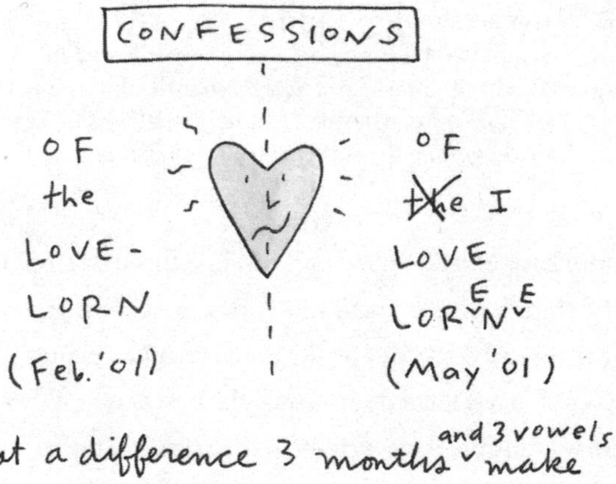

CONFESSIONS

OF the LOVE-LORN (Feb. '01)

OF ~~the~~ I LOVE LORENE (May '01)

What a difference 3 months and 3 vowels make

We hadn't decided that we would live in my house forever. Hers held a hundred years of family history and I was willing to move. But it was a decision we didn't need to make for now. It was more than enough to know that we would spend the rest of our lives together. We planned to have a small civil union in Vermont the next summer, with a big after-party. And sometime before then, we each promised to propose to the other.

HOW DO I PROPOSE to THEE?

We spent the Fourth of July in 2001 at an old farmhouse in Vermont. It had been my college mentor's retreat—no phone, no cell service, no TV. I had been given guest privileges in perpetuity. The weekend was unseasonably cold and rainy, and Lorene and I were wrapped up in a quilt, eating homemade strawberry ice cream in front of a fire. The dogs slept on the couch behind us.

"What are you thinking?" I asked, fishing for something to think about as I stared into the fire, possibly stumbling upon a big thought, like a whole new room in her head.

She took my bowl and set it down, and then she held my hands. "Will you marry me?"

The question took me by surprise; but I didn't have to think about the answer. "I will," I said.

We decided we would be married on that hearth, like the farmers up the road fifty-some years before us.

We met a couple of my old friends for dinner. I was starving by the time we ordered. Barbara smiled at me while we waited for our slices. "You got what you wanted."

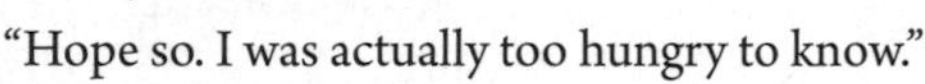

"Hope so. I was actually too hungry to know."

The three of them were laughing. "I meant Lorene and the baby."

> Have you ever thought there were forms of happiness waiting for us to appropriate them by sheer recognition?
>
> Katherine Mosby
> *Private Altars*

As You Wish, Jellyfish

Lorene and I bought copies of *Taking Charge of Your Fertility* and *Alternative Families* and an ovulation predictor kit (OPK). Having a partner added an element of accountability—no chickening out, no procrastination. We studied the books in bed and compiled a list of questions.

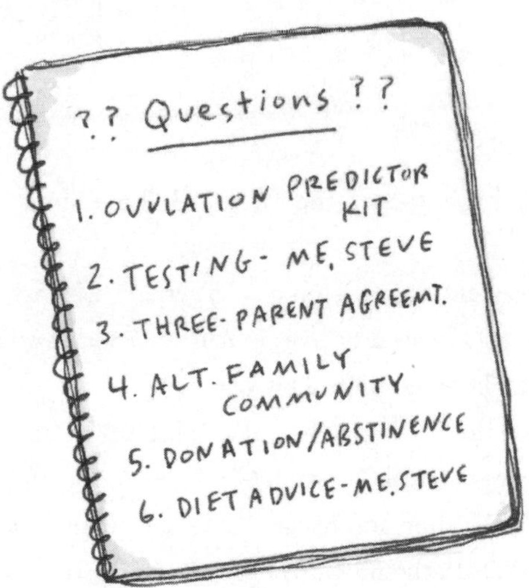

I dug out the notes from the artificial insemination seminar I had attended back when Karen and I were together. It seems I had recorded everything *but* the answers to our questions.

Lorene made an appointment with Liz, the woman who'd run the seminar and the Couples Considering Parenting Support Group. She was standing by a conference table when we arrived. There was a large bag on it, and a speculum and a syringe sitting on top of a folder next to the bag. She introduced herself to Lorene, and the three of us seated ourselves around the bag end of the table.

"Well, how long have you two been together?"

Lorene and I answered at the same time.

Liz smiled and opened the folder. "Tell me about the dad. He's a friend?"

"Steve's an old friend. He's also a writer; we met on vacation in Greece. The tricky part is he lives in Australia, although his job has a lot of flexibility. He travels quite a bit."

"It's great that he's up for it. It's going to be an adventure!" She uncapped her pen. Real Question #1: "Have you figured out how much contact you'd like him and his family to have with your child—in general terms? What's the most? What's the least? These are the kinds of things that go into your agreement."

I answered, "We want to start with the minimum. Whatever Steve thinks he can manage, that way he can always do more over time. We really just don't want him to do less—disappoint the child."

Liz's pen was still poised above the paper, her eyebrows expressing some difficulty in summarizing my answer. "What about the father's financial responsibility?" She skipped down to the next set of lines.

"None. We're going to pay for all the insemination stuff. When there's a real baby, I hope he'll pay for his own travel, to visit . . . "

"Insemination expenses aren't normally covered in a coparenting agreement. It has more to do with visitation rights and financial responsibilities once the baby's born."

"Are there three-parent agreements?" I asked.

"I know of one or two." She gave me the name of the lawyer who had drawn them up.

"All right." Liz was forging on. "Shall we go over insemination?" We nodded. "You've been taking your body temperature? Have you tried the ovulation predictor kit?" We had.

"And have you been watching your cervical mucus?" *Gross. Do I have to?*

INTRODUCING
The
SPECULATOR
(mind if I insert myself?)

NO corner-cutting!

"You want egg-white consistency, clear and stretchy. You can record the amount and quality right on your temperature chart."

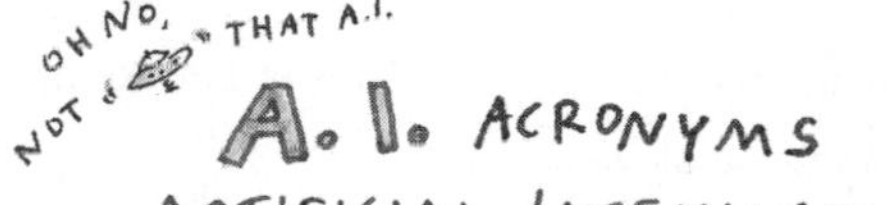

ARTIFICIAL INSEMINATION

BBT - BASAL BODY TEMPERATURE

EWCM - EGG WHITE CONSISTENCY MUCUS

HSG - HYSTEROSALPINGOGRAM (TUBE TEST)

ICI - INTRACERVICAL INSEMINATION

IUI - INTRAUTERINE INSEMINATION

OPK - OVULATION PREDICTOR KIT

Liz unzipped the bag and set a woman's midsection on the table. She turned her upside down and looked to make sure everything was in order. Then she picked up the speculum. Lorene was laughing at me. "You're pink," she said.

"Don't make me red." I was nervous, not embarrassed.

Liz inserted the speculum. "The cervix feels kind of hard, like the tip of your nose." *With egg white on it.* She turned the midriff toward us. "Do you need a speculum?"

"I still have the one we got in the support group," I said.

"Now, you want Steve to abstain for two days before you inseminate. No lubricants other than corn oil. A tall clean glass container works fine for collection." She picked up the syringe. "You take up a little air first—the air helps you get every last bit, and then when your syringe is full, you insert it." She positioned the syringe inside the speculum, which was inside the midriff's hooey. "And that's all there is to it. You can prop Suzy's hips up on some pillows, stay that way for twenty minutes or so." She looked to see if we had any questions.

"I still need to have an HSP—"

"HSG."

"What if one of my tubes is blocked? Do you know what the procedure is, how much time it takes to recover?"

"Cross that bridge when you come to it, and you only need one tube." She smiled and pushed her chair back. "Keep me posted!" It was time for us to go.

The drive home was quiet for a bit, then Lorene blurted out, "If something happens to you, I want custody. I don't want Steve raising our child. I'm the coparent."

"Definitely. I'll call the lawyer tomorrow."

"Oh, God, what if something happens to you? There were times I wish I'd been a better mother to David; I'm lucky he turned out the way he did."

"Everybody makes mistakes." I was grateful for her experience. "Besides, nothing is going to happen to me."

I spoke with the lawyer the next afternoon. She would be happy to draft something; however, she wanted to be up-front about the fact that none of these three-parent agreements had been court tested.

That night I e-mailed Steve the list of tests he'd need to take to screen into a sperm bank and mentioned the coparenting agreement. I wondered whether he could verbalize how much he wanted to be involved as a parent.

> **From:** Steve
> **Subject:** Radical idea
> **Date:** July 13, 2001
>
> It's all really happening, isn't it? It's almost impossible to know where to begin. I figure I'd take a chance and throw a grenade . . .
>
> We've been concocting this wild scheme through e-mails, letters and dreams, and we haven't seen each other for, I don't know, ten years or something. I think we need to get together before we embark on this creative act. If we really want to do it, we need to talk about how it would work and all those thousand questions we both have.
>
> If we go ahead, I'll probably have to come to the States because that's where your doctors are, which means the prelude get-together should be here. Your return trip to Australia—a week, or two—we could book a place in the country, near the sea. It's winter, but it's atmospheric.
>
> There it is, the grenade in the pudding. I haven't changed my mind, I'm not getting cold feet. But this is a pretty big thing we're talking about here and for the sake of Junior, we need to really know what the hell we're doing. What do you think?
>
> Love, Steve XO

The "if we go ahead" landed with a thud in the pit of my stomach. The impossibilities of spending a week away swirled around on top. I was organizing and training for a 5-day, 500-mile bike-a-thon. *How could I do that with no bike, no phone, no Lorene, and who wants to go to Australia during Australian winter?* I called Lorene.

"You have to go."

"I cannot possibly go. Ride FAR—"

"The week after the 50-mile training ride. Want me to look up flights?"

"I don't want to go without you."

Ride FAR was the country's first HIV/AIDS bike-a-thon. Every two years, 25 of us (and 10 land crew) rode 100 miles a day for five days. The ride raised over $1,100,000 for HIV/AIDS service organizations.

"Of course you don't. We have the rest of our lives—*the rest of our lives*—together. You've picked a thoughtful father for your child."

She's right.

Ten days later, I was on a plane heading west. Lorene had draped her compass necklace over my neck at the airport; I held on to it, already missing her. The international dateline would swallow up Sunday, one less day I'd be away, as long as I didn't count the extra Sunday I'd be socked with on the way back.

I slept for ten hours. When I woke up, I took my temperature and entered it into my chart. The pilot announced we were an hour outside of Melbourne. Time to zone in. *What was the zone exactly?* It isn't a sales trip. *Oh, yes it is; I'm not going home without a father.* It is an open-ended preconception retreat.

Not recognizing Steve after ten years skittered across the realm of possibilities as I shuffled through the international-arrivals doors. Then I spotted him raising his cup of coffee, a newspaper folded under his other arm. His hair was a little shorter, more temple showing, but otherwise he looked exactly the same. We hugged, coffee, newspaper, and all. "You still a coffee snob?" he asked.

"Probably worse."

"This one's atrocious. We'll drop your stuff and go straight to a little café in our neighborhood. It's very good—well, you'll tell me what you think."

Steve's street is lined with one- and two-story Australian-Victorian houses. Neat stucco cottages with wood trim, tiled roofs, and well-kept gardens on the other side of garden gates. I was able to pick his out before we parked.

The insides hadn't changed much, although Gary was gone. The two of them had split up a couple years after I'd last seen him. The Greco-inspired murals they had talked about painting over were still intact, but the bedroom beyond the bathroom was empty.

"I just finished cleaning that out last night," Steve said.

"Not for me, I hope . . . "

"No, Mark is moving in the week after you leave." Mark was Steve's new partner.

"Good timing!"

"Yes, I think so. It's a little full on." He laughed. "He's looking forward to meeting you tonight."

After breakfast, we went back home so I could rest and Steve could pack up. We were heading to Fish Creek for our retreat the next morning. I stationed myself on the couch in the living room with an open book on my lap, which gave me the options of reading, napping, or talking while Steve crisscrossed the house, gathering up his belongings.

We talked easily, with the lack of urgency the beginning of a whole week alone together affords two people who haven't seen each other in ten years, especially when one of them does not want to appear overeager. Steve made us toasted cheese and to-mah-to sandwiches in the afternoon. And I drank his homemade apple-carrot-fennel-parsley juice. A true testament to my open preconception mind.

Today's SPECIAL:
Incinerator Back-up Juice

Mark joined us for dinner. Steve met Mark when they were both working for the government. Steve was still working in the same office as a writer. Mark left to get a teaching degree and now taught elementary school. I immediately loved that about him, which completely overrode my preexisting dislike of something he couldn't help—he wasn't Gary.

I waited while Steve walked Mark back to his car; this was their good-bye for the week. As we drove back to Taylor Street, Steve asked, "You sure Lorene is the one?"

"Yeah. It's so easy—I don't know that I can explain it. I don't have to spend any energy meeting her halfway—we're already together."

"It's new."

I blushed in the dark. "She's really nurturing. Her store is like a community center; people go there just to hang out. Everybody loves her." I trailed off, missing Lorene. It would have been so much easier to have her there so he could see she was the one, the way my dad and sisters did.

Steve didn't stir until eleven the next morning. I was up, bags packed, temperature marked on my chart. Turns out there was no need to rush off to Fish Creek; we could head out for a little breakfast and shopping (Fish Creek wouldn't provide any opportunities) on Steve's favorite street. We talked through two coffees and walked the length of the street—in and out of soap and lotion stores, clothing stores, book and paper stores. I ended up with two dog toys for Vita and Mister.

Steve still had more packing to do when we got home, and then there was a stop he'd planned at his parents' house on the way out of town. We would be getting to Fish Creek in time for dinner.

I had the gifts I'd brought for Steve's parents on my lap in the car. Maple syrup and blueberry jam. All of a sudden, they seemed very small. "What do your parents think about this?"

"June's intrigued. She never expected to get a grandchild out of me. And Pete has always really liked you—he's quite impressed with your books. He hasn't tuned in to the baby thing."

I was starving by the time we arrived. June's buttery toasted cheese-and-tomato sandwiches tasted delicious. She had collected photos from Steve's boyhood to show us. After lunch, Steve sat with his dad. I stood with June while she refilled her bird feeder with brown sugar and water. Wild parrots fluttered around the patio off her kitchen. I could see a lot of Steve in her face. I read the hint of a smile as acceptance. We could have been mother- and daughter-in-law, the two of us standing there talking.

After a bit, Steve and I traded places. I joined Pete at his desk on the enclosed porch, his retirement office. Stacks of unfiled folders were piled on the tops of full filing cabinets. We talked about publishing and the economy. "Has Steve shown you the elementary school?" he asked, looking up at me over his half glasses. "It's right at the end of the street; the boys walked there from here. They spent a lot of time at the little creek you'll pass on the way."

Steve took me down to the school, stopping by the dried-up creek where he and Andrew had played. After we got back, we corralled June and Pete together on the front doorstep for a couple of photos, then left for Fish Creek.

It was dark when we pulled in. We threw our bags into our separate rooms and Steve changed into his "house pants"—a familiar pair of now grayed-out blue "track" pants with white stripes down the sides. He put some music on and got dinner started. His meals are simple, just a few ingredients—in this case, pasta, tomato, and mushrooms—but he enjoys laboring over them. He was singing, chopping, sautéing, and stirring alone in the kitchen for over an hour. I read my book on the couch.

Neither of us made any mention of a baby—the retreat didn't officially begin until the next day.

After dinner, we went for a walk. The sky was full of stars, pinhole pricks of bright light, no moon. There was a chorus of cud chewing; once our eyes adjusted, we could make out a hundred or more dark blobs in the meadow alongside the road.

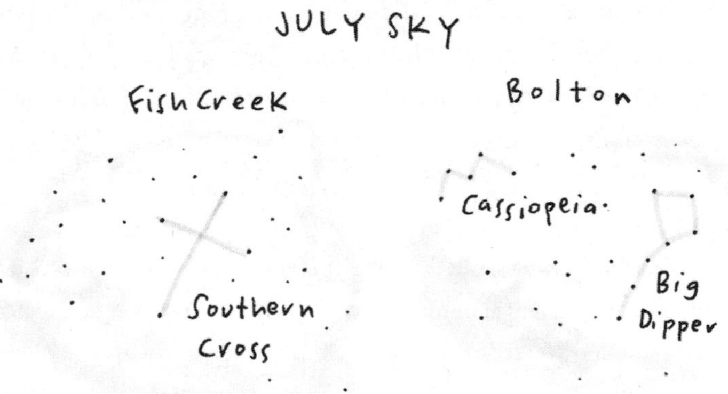

"The sky's so different. Must be upside-down."

"Different for me, too; I'm not used to being here in winter," Steve said. "I don't think you ever get the Southern Cross."

note to SELF

2. Learn constellations before child is of star-gazing age.

1. Learn star-gazing age.

Steve made himself a cup of tea, and I said good night. I fell asleep to strains of techno-pop music and his occasional throat clearing as he worked on his novel. I awoke the next morning at six (the dogs' breakfast hour) and recorded my temperature. Day 13 of my cycle. I should be ovulating any day now. I would wait until after lunch to break out the predictor kit.

Steve got out of bed at nine and made his morning tea. I let him wake up, appearing immersed in my writing. *I was thinking we could start the retreat off with a real bang* . . . We had talked about the possibility of just jumping into bed together, circumventing the rest of the process. Everyone, including Lorene and Mark, was in favor of the concept.

We went to the Flying Cow for breakfast. The café was two doors down from our place. The owner was eight and a half months pregnant. "Where's Mark?" she greeted Steve.

"He's leaving us to work out this part of the project," Steve answered.

"Please, don't make me laugh," she begged, and steadied her middle.

We sat down and ordered "flat white" coffees, bacon, and eggs. "I thought you were a vegetarian," Steve said.

People always do—it must have to do with my writing animal books or my earnestness or something. "Nope, but I hardly ever eat red meat."

"I am," Steve said. "I'll eat a little chicken, if Mark's cooking, and it's hard to get around eating lamb in this country."

Our breakfast arrived. We were the only ones in the place. "Weather's not so good. I thought maybe we'd go to Foster this afternoon, do a supermarket shop."

"I need to do this tester thing before we go; I think I'm getting ready to ovulate."

He laughed nervously. "Well, that makes things interesting. I suppose we could stay home and spend the afternoon in bed. Is that what you were thinking?"

"I'd be tomorrow or the next day, if it's positive." I paused. "I don't know, when we used to talk about it, I always imagined the other two nearby. Feels like there should be some ground rules—"

"Shirts on, lights on. No, lights off!" We were laughing. "No, you're right, it could be dangerous. What if we like it? How about we agree to do it just once . . . " He shifted in his chair. "I'm sure you've thought about it. I've thought about it . . . "

"I have. I—well, if we were both single . . . In this stupid, idealistic way, I always wanted this whole thing to be an act of love, not—not turkey baster or technology."

I paid for breakfast and we left. "We don't have to decide right now," he said. "Do your test. We *could* call home." The phone was in front of the post office, on the other side of our place.

"I don't want to wake Lorene. I know what she'd say—'Go for it!'"

"Same with Mark."

We walked into the post office. Steve made a copy of his sperm-test results. I bought ten postcard stamps.

"As you wish, jellyfish," the clerk said, and handed me the stamps in a little sleeve.

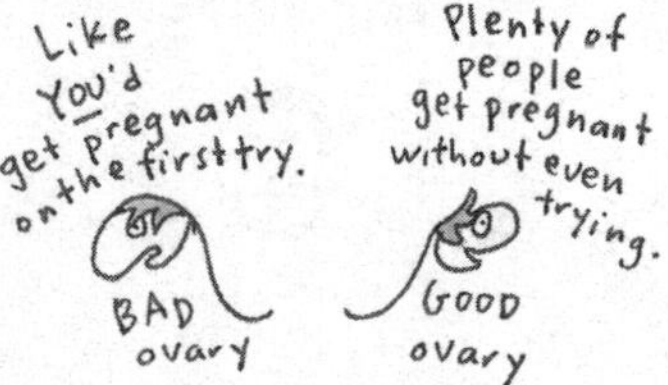

What *did* I wish? I wished for a baby. I wished Lorene was there. All of a sudden I had this strong feeling that I didn't want her to miss the Moment.

When we got back, we each took a seat at the dining room table, our notebooks in front of us in place of place mats. "You go first," Steve said. "I realized I don't really have that many questions. I guess the trip itself was kind of a test balloon . . . I think I just needed to know how it would feel, to make sure, after all these years. Yeah. So I don't have specific questions. I'm sure I will have them, after you go."

"Okay, the first question. Have you given more thought to how much of a father you want to be?"

"Yeah. The distance is tough . . . My best friend Kelly sees his kids a few times a year. I was thinking once a year, at least. Maybe alternate, here, there, somewhere in between. What were you thinking?"

"Like that. With calls, letters, e-mail . . . Whatever we decide, I just want to make sure we can really do it. I don't want to set the kid up for disappointment. And I want to celebrate birthdays and Christmas—"

"Together?"

"No, long distance. But they'd be important."

"Definitely." We stared at our notebooks. "Would you want me there for the birth?" he asked.

"Not a command performance. If you'd want to be there, I'd love it. I think. I have no idea what it'll be like."

"Who knows with any of this stuff? We should be allowed to change our minds . . ."

"Except lowering the minimums on involvement."

"Okay, here's another one for you, then," Steve said. "What if I fall in love at the birth, you know, with the baby, and decide I want to stay?"

"Fine. Just not in our house."

"Next door?"

"Great. Here's one for you. What if she hates us when she's fourteen and she wants to come live with you?"

"Seriously?"

"I hope not."

"That'd be just about perfect timing for me. I love high school kids." Steve paused, then said, "My friends all think this is crazy. They keep saying—maybe it's because of your brain surgery—'Something's going to happen to Suzy and Junior's going to land on your doorstep.'"

"Lorene would get custody of Junior. Or do you mean if something happened to both of us? I was going to make my younger sister Meredith guardian in the will. You'd have visitation—would you want Junior?"

He thought for a bit. "I think you're right . . . "

We talked through lunch and then I took my OPK into the bathroom. Steve raised his eyebrows when I came out. "It takes five minutes."

We stood beholding the stick. Steve put his hand on my shoulder. "Darling, if we were going to be really responsible, I should have all my test results, right? The hep C results aren't back yet."

"That settles it?"

"I think so."

"Could you possibly have hep C?"

"I don't know. Let's go to Foster."

When I woke up the next morning, I reached for my purple thermometer. 97.1 degrees, the telltale drop. *If we were going to do it, this would be the day.*

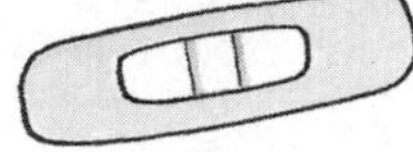

Ovulation Predictor Kit (OPK)

The test detects the surge in luteinizing hormone (produced in the morning) which separates the egg from the follicle. Fertilization occurs 1 to 3 days later, 36 hours optimally.

The sun was out and so was our hot water, a conclusion I reached four minutes into a cold shower. I dried off, got dressed, and went down to the post office to buy a phone card. It was Bruce's birthday.

"Nice place that, where you're staying?" Mrs. Jellyfish inquired.

"It's perfect for us, just no hot water this morning." I offered up the intimate detail since this was our second meeting.

"It's a chilly morning. Not as bad as yesterday. Tell your friend there to ring the owner up." I was surprised she didn't say "husband."

I left Bruce a singing message, then tried Lorene. Just a quick call to tell her I loved her, missed her, and we weren't going to do it.

"Do you want to?"

"Kind of. If I got pregnant and we could skip the rest."

"You still could . . ."

"I don't want to bring it up again. Maybe when he's there in the fall."

RELIEF — I don't have to   ? < > =   WISH — I could

She didn't sound 10,000 miles away. "You okay?" I asked.

"I'm okay. The house is okay. Mister and Vita are okay. We miss you, but we're fine. You okay?"

"I am. Feels selfish, though. I wish you were here."

"It's not selfish. It's a wonderful thing you're doing."

Steve was padding down the walk in his house pants. "No hot water! I'm going to phone the guy."

We adjusted our routine and headed to the Flying Cow. The owner looked up from her copy of the Fish Creek *Mirror*. "Heard your hot water heater's stuffed. You're welcome to shower in the back here."

I turned to Steve. "Wait, how does she know?"

Steve shook his head and started laughing. "Small town, this."

After breakfast we discussed finances and football. I would pay for all of the donation expenses and any of Steve's testing that wasn't covered under his insurance. He insisted on paying for his travel, including the sperm-banking trip. Aside from visiting, he wouldn't have any further financial responsibility, which raised the topic of citizenship. Steve didn't feel strongly, but if the baby were an Australian citizen, "uni"—university, our biggest foreseeable future outlay—would be free.

I segued to school in general. I felt strongly about sending the kid to public school. Steve wasn't set on anything. He had been the equivalent of an American public high school teacher and graduated from the public schools, but he had seen friends' kids benefit from private schooling.

"How much do you want to be a part of those kinds of decisions?"

"However much is useful. Parenting's already tricky between two people, I don't know that you want a third. But I'm happy to weigh in when you want. How's that?"

"Good. What about football?" Lorene was opposed, I was pro—not pushing it, but if our kid wanted to play.

Steve didn't know the first thing about American football, so he refused to cast the tie-breaking vote, saying instead, "Those things will usually sort themselves out."

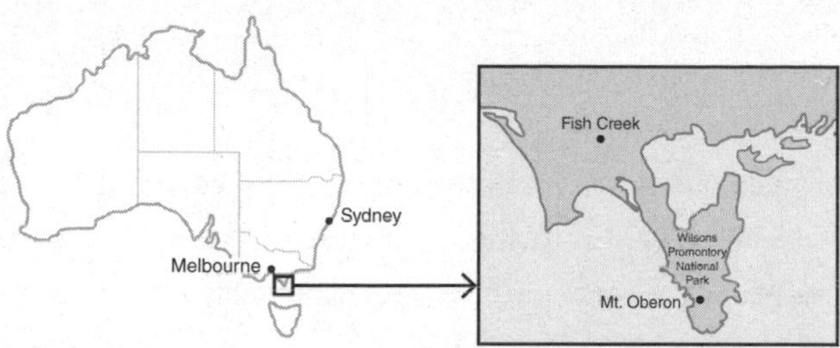

Enough for one day. Still no sign of the hot-water man. We packed up a lunch and left for Wilsons Promontory, the southernmost tip of Australia. We picnicked on top of Mount Oberon, looking out over the Southern Ocean.

"Do you want a girl or a boy?" Steve asked.

Coincidentally, I had just been reading about how to control the sex of the baby during conception that morning.

"I don't know. Sometimes I think I was better with the boys when I was teaching, and then I think maybe it'd be harder for a boy to be raised by two women—but it's not like there won't be men in our kid's life . . . Did you talk to your dad about sex?"

Steve let out a mini-shriek. "Good God, neither of them. I remember a dinner party when I must have been about twelve, they virtually shut me in my room with a book about the birds and the bees. Literally. I remember there were swans, strange images of swans . . . "

Natural

SEX SELECTION

Girl sperm is larger, slower, and lives longer than boy sperm. On average, sperm live 3 to 5 days in a woman's body. The egg lives 1 to 2 days after being released. Trying to get pregnant *before* ovulation improves the girl sperm's odds; trying later gives boy sperm the advantage.

OR: Consult the *Ancient Chinese Predictor Chart* which uses your age to identify boy or girl conception-months with 93% accuracy.

B	G	B	G	B	G	B	G	B	G	B	G

"What about you? Boy or girl?"

"I'm like you. Either, really."

I stretched out on the rocks with my eyes closed, imagining Steve introducing his kid to his friends, then woke up twenty minutes later. Steve was peering down at me. "We should probably head down if you want to do that river walk," he said.

We walked along the Darby River out to the ocean. I did the driving on the way back in the dusk, completely comfortable on the left side of the carless roads.

WILDLIFE SIGHTINGS

WOMBAT	𝍸
EMU	I
WALLABY	I
SWAMP WALLABY	I

The hot water was fixed. I had a shower and half a glass of red wine and fell asleep while Steve made dinner. Steve had a gin and tonic and wanted to talk all night. We took turns playing our CDs, filling each other in on the past ten years. Then we talked about writing. Steve finally let me fall asleep reading one of his travel pieces.

By the third day, we were about out of questions. Steve's notebook was shut, his pen sitting on top, his hands in his pockets.

I had one more. "Have you thought about how you want to do the sperm-banking? Will Mark be able to come along with you? West Coast, East Coast?"

"Mark can't get vacation time when school's in session. The West Coast might be nice. You'd come there?"

"I could. I don't think Lorene could be there the whole time, but part of it."

Steve looked at me strangely. "We're doing it, we're really going to do this, aren't we?" We took an unscheduled hug break, after which neither one of us wanted to return to the table.

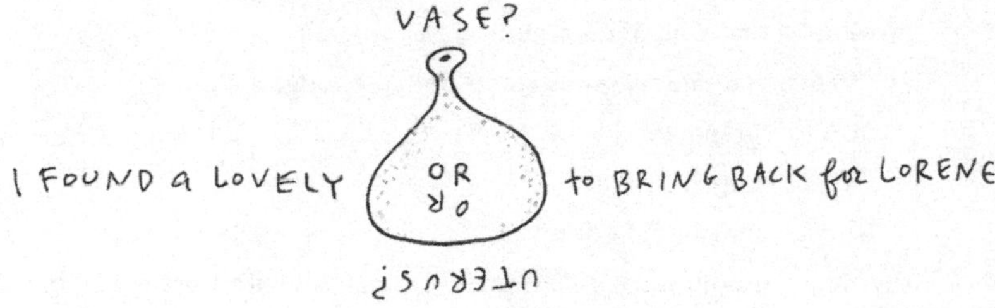

That afternoon we walked down a jetty in another deserted fishing village. The jetty, a landmark from Steve's childhood, was the draw. By the time we showed up at the town bar, they were done serving lunch. Steve wheedled two toasted cheese sandwiches out of a closed kitchen, then sat down with a surprisingly sheepish look.

"Everything okay?" I asked.

"Me? Yeah. No, you know, it's weird. There was something you said once. It was during one of our phone conversations"—*something I said, something I said*—"and I keep coming back to it. I'm not sure what you meant—and I guess it's the only, well, I guess it's a concern, not a question."

The toasted cheeses were delivered, prolonging my agony. "A concern?"

"I don't know if you'll remember saying it, and now I can't remember the context . . . " *Out with it already!* "You said you wanted to raise the child in a religious community, and I was wondering what type—"

"Oh, okay." I'd cut him off. I didn't mean to belittle or, worse, aggravate his concern. "Lorene's son loved being part of the local Unitarian church—a pretty liberal, social-activist, I guess you'd call it Christian religion. But that church has changed a lot. If we could find another good Unitarian church close by, with a community of people—the kind you bring dinner for or they bring dinner for you—we'd like our kid to grow up in that kind of community."

"When you said religious community, I thought—"

"Cult." We laughed.

"That's really it."

The last morning, I got up early to run along the beach before I did the eighteen-hour plane ride home. My final call with Lorene had been unnerving.

We had been together only two months. It was silly to think our reserves would span six days, across half of the world. Tomorrow we would begin replenishing them. *We'll have the rest of our lives . . . and a baby together.*

DOING O.K. (Days 1-5) ← fine line

DOING just FINE (Day 6) without you, thanks.

I took Lorene's compass necklace from my neck and put it around Steve's at the airport. "For your trip."

"Sure you don't want it for yours?"

"Nah, it got me here, now it'll bring you back." We hugged good-bye and I headed for customs. I turned to wave one last time before I passed through the double doors.

The Best Laid Plans

Lorene and I stayed up all night (or morning or whatever time it was according to my body's clock) catching up when I got home and slept in the next morning. She had not received a single postcard from Fish Creek.

There were flowers all over—in the kitchen, on the nightstand, in both bathrooms. There were books left open on couches, more books on the tables, and piles of CDs on the player. A history of the time I'd been away.

Most of the rest of August was taken up with work and training for Ride FAR. September's ride ended up raising more than $120,000. We had five days of sun, 500 miles without injury or a single bike breakdown.

The first morning after the ride, Lorene stared me awake. She was sitting up in our bed. The second my eyes opened, she announced, "I feel like I'm home. *This* is my home now." We floated through the day, on a cloud of post-Ride, day-off, early-September sunny euphoria. But the next morning, we came crashing down.

Bruce called while we were having breakfast. All he said was, "Go turn on your TV." We were watching over the tops of our knees by the time the plane hit the second tower. *Never doubt that a small group . . . can change the world . . .*

The third plane hit the Pentagon. The fourth plane crashed in Pennsylvania. It was days before we stopped anticipating news of a fifth, sixth, and seventh plane. And I don't know that any of us of a certain age will ever permanently put that possibility to rest.

"I don't think I want to bring a baby into this world," I told Lorene.

"It's too soon, too soon to tell," she answered me.

> **From:** Steve
> **Subject:** At my 12th floor desk
> **Date:** September 17, 2001
>
> Hi Honey, It's late, it's dark and I'm at work (in a high rise), half listening for the door-click as the cleaner comes in. I really need to connect with you. I'd be lying if I said I wasn't afraid of getting on a plane just now. The Boston–L.A. path has a touch of the freaky about it. There's also the uncertainty about what happens next in the world. Where will this terrorism have led us in a month's time? Don't worry, I'm not getting cold feet—funny, I've realized over the last few weeks how much I do want to do this baby thing with you. I've also reflected a bit on what if it doesn't work, and that reminds me how much I do want it to work, but like we've said, there are lots of other adventures ahead.
>
> So, how are you feeling? If we delayed, how far would it set us back?
>
> Love you, Suzy. More than ever, Steve

A month later, we were beginning to trust a blue sky again. We had held babies and felt hope surface again.

> My heart is moved by all I cannot save:
> so much has been destroyed
>
> I have cast my lot with those
> who age after age, perversely,
>
> with no extraordinary power,
> reconstitute the world.
>
> ADRIENNE RICH
> *"Natural Resources"*

From: Suzy
Subject: Re: At my 12th floor desk
Date: October 21, 2001

Let's do December! Christmas in New England, and your birthday! If we're trying for two cycles, I'd be ovulating December 1st and January 1st, so it'd be good if you arrived in late November; although, as Lorene pointed out, after that carwash I gave her for her birthday, the backseat is clean enough, we could do it on the way home from the airport! I watched the news while I was on jury duty yesterday; they're now projecting a national stress-induced baby boom. Back to our Sunday. We're excited again. (Please see exclamation points above.)
Love, Suzy

The nice thing (not the *only* nice thing) about having houseguests is that they give a to-do list a deadline.

Three days before Steve arrived, I was scheduled to have the test to make sure my tubes were clear (see #6 on list). My gynecologist was running late. I was on the table with my knees up when she brushed by Lorene, gloved up, lifted my gown, and shook her head, disgusted.

I had forgotten to take off my underwear. I scooched out of them and flung them over to Lorene, which had my gynecologist hissing, blowing a gasket–like, "If those had landed on my tray, we would've had to start all over with the sterile prep." Needless to say, she had no time for that. From where I was, in the stirrups, it was hard to imagine further humbling yourself, but I apologized. And she got to work.

Left tube: clear! Right tube: *Jesusfuckingchrist!* I arched my back off the table. Lorene took a few steps toward me. The gynecologist gave the dye another go. "Let's try this again," she said. *If having a baby is more painful than this, I may resign.* "I don't know whether it is blocked or spasming. There was a nice pool—you saw the way the dye came through the other tube?"

She was talking to Lorene and motioning at the monitor hanging up over my left shoulder. Lorene nodded; she was holding my hand. "There's no reason why that other tube should be blocked. These spasms can take thirty minutes to calm down."

"What if it *is* blocked?" Lorene asked.

"You'd run the risk of a tubal or ectopic pregnancy."

"How are those treated?"

"Laparoscopy." She removed her gloves. "I have to run."

I crumpled up my gown and threw it away. Having a baby seemed so unlikely again. I had stupidly let my hopes get carried away with Steve's arrival preparations. "Hey," Lorene said, looping her arm through mine. "Remember? You only need one."

The air-duct cleaning (see #5) backfired on us. A small pile of dust on top of the oil burner caught fire and blew smoke all over the house. At the end of the day (less than forty-eight hours before our chemically sensitive Australian guest was due), we had clean ducts and a house that stunk like an ashtray. "At least there's no dog smell," Lorene observed. No dog smell. No wood-smoke smell. No coffee smell. Not a hint of the spaghetti sauce that had cooked all day for last night's dinner. Just ashtray. "Well, what're you going to do." It wasn't a question (we had done everything that we could think of); that's what Lorene said when the answer was "nothing."

Steve's flight touched down a few minutes after midnight on November 28th. We met at the curb and exchanged quick hugs. "We should have brought you a down jacket—I have a big one at home you can borrow," Lorene said as we loaded him into our Civic. The two of them fell into easy conversation while I concentrated on finding today's way out of Logan Airport.

There was a silence in the tunnel; Lorene volunteered, "We're waiting to get a new car until we know whether we're going to get a baby. Probably something with four doors."

"And two visors," I added, all of a sudden seeing the car through Steve's eyes.

The Charles River came into view, lit up on both sides. The night seemed unusually clear and welcoming. Full of promise.

"Our Ride FAR friend Mary Ann is coming in the morning," I began.

"Noon," Lorene continued. "Mary Ann's a delivery nurse—she delivers babies out in the western part of the state."

"She offered to show us how to do everything."

"Oh?" Steve shifted in his seat.

"Suzy should be ovulating any day now," Lorene volunteered.

"Good on you!" he patted my leg. *I hope he teaches our baby, if we have a baby, all of his Aussie expressions.*

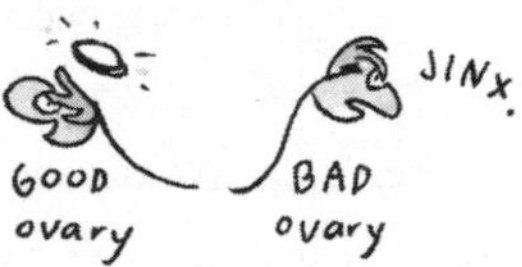

"Good on *you*!" I returned the pat. "Your timing is pretty perfect."

The barn light illuminated the white picket fence and the winter remnants of the garden along the walk up to the kitchen door. We had recounted our air-duct minidrama during the last part of the ride, so Steve was obliged to comment. "It doesn't smell too bad," he said politely.

Given the hour and the next day's agenda, we all agreed to turn in. "Hope you won't mind my bumping around in the middle of the night," Steve said. "I get terrible insomnia coming in this direction." We got him settled in his room and gave him a quick tour of the house.

INSOMNIAC'S TOUR HIGHLIGHTS

"He's great!" Lorene said once we were in bed. "I don't know what I expected—he's completely regular." The way she said it made being regular sound exceptional.

The next morning, Lorene and I had breakfast and went to work as usual. Steve was sleeping. There was some evidence—a mug of unfinished tea, an open magazine on the kitchen table—of insomnia. He was still sleeping when Lorene came home just before noon. She had a bunch of purple irises: "These are for you, O my beloved, O the delight of my eyes." She was channeling Rudyard Kipling again. The words had run through her head for months before she felt comfortable saying them; now she came out with them every few days. "They didn't have the white ones. They're for the beginning."

So *this* was the beginning.

I was still looking for something to put them in when Mary Ann arrived. She was predictably pink-faced (although usually it's from the cycling, not the cold) and high-spirited, which could also account for some of the pink. She let herself in, predictably no-nonsense. "Where's Steve?" she asked.

Steve entered on cue. Semi-dressed (not half nude), wearing his house pants, uncombed and unshaven. "Strange night," he said after he and Mary Ann had been introduced. "Anyone else care for a cup of tea?"

Mary Ann had a cup. We stood around the kitchen, the two of them sipping tea. "How'd you sleep, Steve?" Lorene asked.

"Well, you'll never believe this," Steve laughed. "Most bizarre thing, I don't know that I could tell you the last time . . . I had a wet dream."

Dare I ask:

(a) *How much of a wet dream: half, three quarters, the whole wad?*

(b) *Wow, what was it about?*

(c) *Who's that in the garden?*

There was a man with a ladder in the garden, tromping on the plants, eyeing the roof above our bedroom.

"Hello?" I called out.

"Mrs. Becker? You called about your chimney?"

I closed the door. "I called him *five* months ago—I gave up on him four months ago. *TODAY* is the day he's going to set his ladder up outside our bedroom window? Perfect!"

Steve and Mary Ann were cracking up. Lorene went to find a sheet to tack up over our naked window. By the time she returned, the guy was packing up. Mary Ann set her mug in the kitchen sink and said, "Well, shall we?"

SMALL SOUFFLE CUP

I took one of my mother's white soufflé cups out of the cabinet and presented it to Steve. Then we filed upstairs, leaving Steve at his bedroom door, next door to ours.

Mary Ann laid out her equipment on the bed. A flashlight, speculum, and a small syringe with a flexible plastic catheter tube on the end. Lorene took a closer look at the syringe while I dropped my drawers and got into bed. The three of us chatted like normal people with pants on, waiting for Steve's delivery. His knock startled us. "It's not much," he apologized.

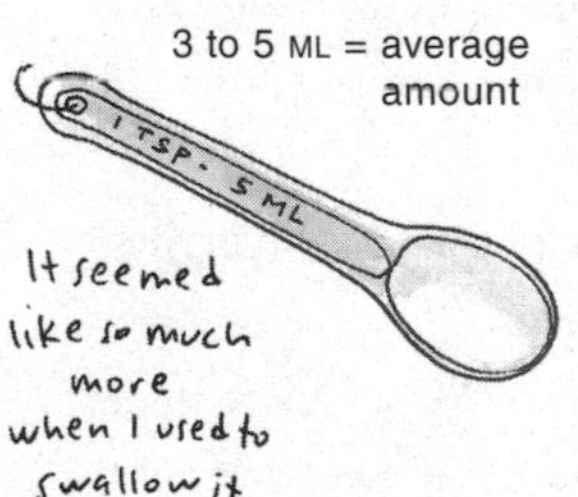

"It's fine. Thank you," Lorene said, and gently shut the door on him. She tipped the cup to show Mary Ann.

"Not bad," Mary Ann said. "After that story downstairs, I wasn't sure what we'd get. You only need one, right?"

Mary Ann had Lorene insert the speculum. She suctioned up Steve's offering with the syringe, took aim, and pushed the plunger.

Lorene propped my hips up on a couple of pillows and kissed my belly. Mary Ann patted it, hugged Lorene goodbye, chirped, "I want to be the fourth to know!" and she was gone.

Lorene left the door open. "Steve?" Steve padded in and the three of us hung out until I was sure the sperm had made it down to my sinuses. Then we went downstairs to make dinner.

Over the next couple of days, Steve settled in. Having him around during the day instantly made working alone less lonely. I anticipated the shuffling of moccasins across the kitchen floor (~10:30), overtaken by a combination of whistling and humming, overtaken by the orange juicer, the teakettle whistling and shaking, followed by a silence of varying length as he read during his breakfast, invariably punctuated by an endearing shriek—Mister or Vita had found an exposed ankle or hand to lick—then, "Okay, all right, yes, we're going to be friends."

He would be at his desk working on his novel by the time I came down for lunch. Then, when he was ready for a break, he'd call upstairs and the two of us would take the dogs for a long walk.

We had another couple of soufflé cup sessions over those next two nights. And we mixed up our routine. Night 1, we tried Advice #2 (about as exciting as it looks spelled out). Night 2, Steve, self-proclaimed urban shaman, did the laying-on of hands.

I observed the same hands dropping everything they came into contact with the next day; Steve was still in the grips of his jet lag insomnia. On Night 3, when I made mention of a patch of soapsuds on the drying dishes, he threw down his sponge and left the kitchen. I apologized when he came back an hour later to make himself some tea. "It's all right," he said, hyperfocused on the tea. "I guess it's the first time I wondered what kind of mother you'll really be. You're very critical."

It was my turn to leave the room. I went to bed. I was still reading when Lorene came up. "Hey, do you feel pregnant?"

"I don't feel any different." I thought about it. "Maybe sometimes I feel a slight something on my right side. It's only been a few days. Why, when did you first feel pregnant?"

"The next day. I remember taking the mail out of the mailbox and I knew—but then I never felt like that again. I wouldn't believe it until I heard his heartbeat."

Our exchange prompted an informal survey of my mother friends: "When and how did you know you were pregnant?" More than half of my respondents admitted to being clueless or wrong. The others gave the following prenatal symptoms: big boobs, feeling tired, bloated, and/or hormonal, getting a zit, peeing more often. With the exception of the last one, they all sounded pretty premenstrual to me.

I asked my mother.

I woke up with my period on December 16th, two days before Steve's birthday. It *would* have made the best present. I sat in the bathroom and looked out toward the woods. Everything looked so black-and-white. *And red.* I went back to bed and told Lorene.

"It's just the first try," she said, and rolled me into her.

We tiptoed past Steve's room. I made waffles while Lorene got a fire going in the wood stove. We were reading the Sunday paper when Steve came down. He toted his bag of oranges over to the cutting board.

I brought my plate to the sink and turned to face him. "I just got my period."

"Ohhh, honey." He held my shoulders. "Never mind." He gave me a big hug and went back to his oranges. "Juice? C'mon, lots of—"

"VITTamins," Lorene joined in from across the room.

Never mind. Never mind, never mind, never mind. It has to be one of the kindest things anyone's ever said.

A Bad Chapter

Back in August, the three of us had decided to go with an instate sperm bank over the California competitor. Convenience beat conviviality. We had filled out all the paperwork. Steve had passed all the tests in advance (they had waived their upper age limit), and we were screened in for the "anonymous" donor program, which doubled as their "selected" (as in unwed to donee) donor program.

Anonymous Donors
a.k.a. altruistic men willing to "help couples experience the joy of conceiving a child"

aka College dudes getting paid $100 to wank off.

I called the bank the morning after I got my period (the day before Steve's birthday) and made our first appointment.

A week later, we were standing in front of a flat concrete-and-brick building, breathing through our coat collars, attempting to verify the building number on the other side of the people smoking. We crossed a dimly lit lobby and got onto a dimly lit elevator. There was still a chance the place would be gleaming and futuristic, on a secret, hermetically sealed floor, until the elevator doors opened. A man obscured another dimly lit floor.

	– 35	eggs per day
×	7	days
	– 245	eggs

"Suzy, Stephen? Tom Mecke!" He threw out his hand and I shook it as I stepped off the elevator. There was something Oz-like about the welcome, a bushy-brown-eyebrowed director doubling as doorkeeper. Mecke led us down a short corridor by the lab, which was visible through the windows on our left. (The windows on our right were painted a

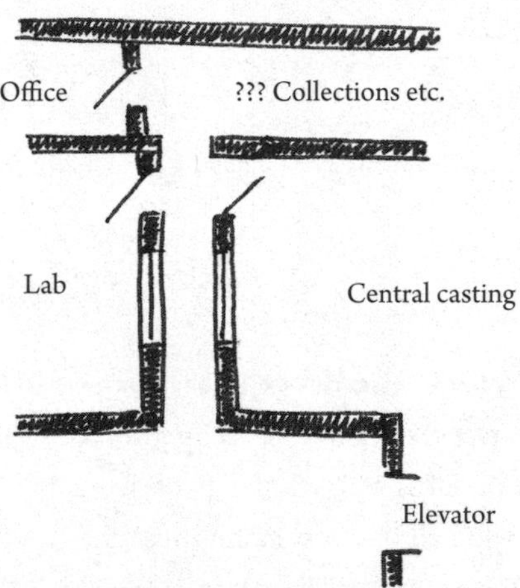

mysterious milky blue, with a matching unmarked milky-blue door. He put on a white coat with a royal-blue cursive *Director* emblazoned on the left breast as we entered a small office. Mecke gestured to the now-empty coat tree. Steve and I hung up our coats and sat down. He opened the one folder, presumably ours, sitting on the empty desk, looked up at us, and launched into his welcome spiel. Every sentence seemed to contain the word "family." It was holding up in all the different contexts—his family, our family, the family-run operation, part of the center's family—and then it started to warp from overuse and the eyebrows dialed up a memory of that fertility doctor who fathered all the clients' children.

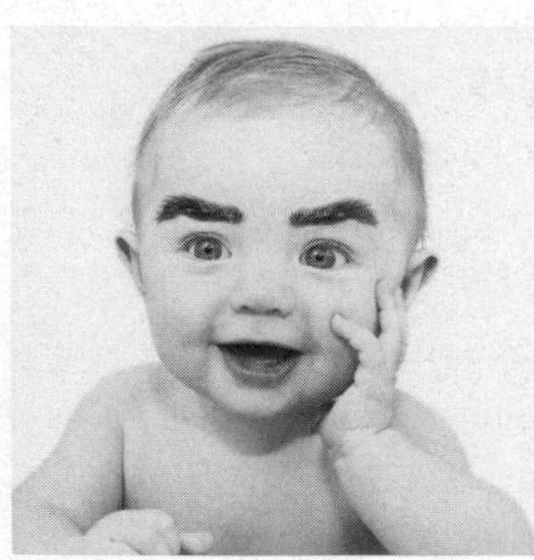

" . . . and now *you* must have some questions for me." The eyebrows were on Steve. Steve looked at me.

My questions were so unfamilial. Bankerly. "Well, how often can Steve make a, a deposit?"

"We recommend waiting two days in between specimen collections."

I got out my calendar. "Will we have enough after eight collections? We had been thinking twelve"—a year's worth of tries—"since he lives in Australia."

"It all depends how much Stephen produces, and the quality of the specimen." The two men exchanged looks; Steve's eyebrows were junior–bushy league. "We recommend at least two collections." He looked through the folder. "Are we preparing these for intracervical or intrauterine insemination?" He paused. "Never mind, we've gotten ahead of ourselves here. Let's have you meet with the doctor, Suzy, and we'll have Stephen produce his specimen, then we'll know exactly what we're talking about."

He handed me a folding chair and motioned toward the hallway as he led Steve off to the collection room. I unfolded the chair and set up with my back to the lab, angling for a glimpse into the milky-blue beyond. Ten minutes went by, nothing doing. Then a kindly-looking old man with wispy white hair came out of the office/collection area. I half stood to let him by, he half bowed in my direction, and we nearly banged heads. "I'm Dr. Felton. You're Suzy?" I nodded. "I've just spoken with Stephen. I left him in there to—" his voice trailed off as he glanced up and down the hallway. "Well, this looks pretty private," he said, unfolding himself a chair.

DR. FELTON

"Stephen and I went over all of his test results and his medical history. Has he shared any of this?" he held up the questionnaire. I nodded and he went on, "Then you're aware Stephen"—*is gay. Yes, and I*—"had an undescended testicle?" *And now so is everyone in hearing distance.*

Steve had actually mentioned it, under the heading of things he didn't know until he had to fill out that questionnaire. "It was fixed," I said, "operated on when he was one."

My intimate knowledge impressed Dr. Felton enough for him to confide in me, "I have met some women who are *so* picky about their donors—I've been tempted to ask them, 'Did you bother to ask your husband whether he was fertile before you married him?'" I smiled understandingly. *I* wasn't one of those women.

Dr. Felton leafed though the rest of Steve's packet, making passing reference to some heart and thyroid disease—all very common within an extended family. "I think we're all set here," he said when he got to the end. He smiled, rose, did another half bow in closing, then walked back to wherever it was he had come from. The heating system rumbled on in his wake—the HVAC opposite of the whir of a cryogenic cooling system—then rumbled off after he'd disappeared.

I kept my eyes fixed on the opening, willing Steve to reappear. *It didn't take him this long at home!* I was studying the plaques above the doorway when Steve walked through, shaking his head. We refrained from further conversation until we were in the privacy of the elevator. "Well"—I couldn't tell from looking at him—"how was it?"

"A blond Britney Spears type with a caveman—an unattractive caveman—"

"They only had *one* video?"

"No, it was the newest one. The doctor recommended it."

"Wait, you don't think he screens—"

"Mmm. It would seem he does. Well, I hope it went all right. It's all very odd, really. I've never had to fuss about these things before..." He zipped up his coat. "And how was your interview?

'Stephen, you've had sex with men,'" he imitated Dr. Felton halfheartedly. "Does Suzy know?"

"Nope, nothing on that. He asked if I knew about your undescended testicle."

"Good God."

The lab didn't have Steve's sperm analysis the next morning. The receptionist picked up on my urgency. "Is your husband going in for chemo, Mrs. Dillon?" We *were* new to the agency family.

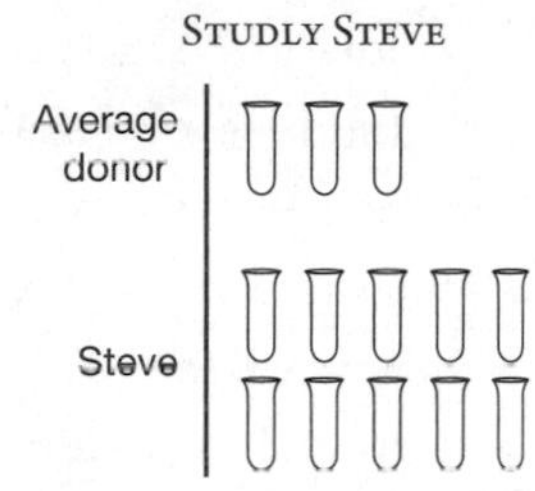

"Oh, no, he's just going back to Australia. We're trying to get his appointments set up." She had no further questions. That afternoon she called back. "Ten dense vials with 96% motility fresh, 87% frozen," I repeated aloud, although Steve had heard through the phone, and threw my arm around his waist.

The receptionist scheduled appointments, one every three days through the end of December.

We called Lorene with the good news. "So are we celebrating?" she asked.

"Steve's spending the night at Bruce's. They're going porn shopping. You and I were going to decorate the tree . . . "

It was our first Christmas together but none of it was shaping up the way I had imagined. It was all my imagination's fault: People in retail (Lorene, for example) don't celebrate Christmas, they survive it. She had to work late, trying to keep up with the framing orders. And people from Australia (Steve, for instance) don't care about making cookies or hanging stockings by a fireplace—it's 95 degrees in Melbourne this time of year.

That night, Lorene and I didn't get to decorate the tree. We had a quiet dinner and toasted "to Daddy's sperm."

"Just think," Lorene said, "this time next year, you could be pregnant."

"But we still have one more try while Steve's here . . . " *This is the kind of thinking that sets someone up for disappointment.*

I picked Steve's head out, bobbing toward me, almost a block away. Funny how you can go years without seeing someone, then miss him when you're apart for a night. "Porn mission accomplished?" I asked, pointing to the backpack. He nodded.

This time a woman from the lab greeted us at the elevators. There wasn't a proper reception area or a receptionist. She instructed us to wait while she disappeared back into the lab.

Steve whispered, "Strange characters, this place." I nodded. She reappeared and led Steve down the hall.

Steve's second deposit went much faster. In fact, it took him longer to pick a pound of handmade chocolates on the way home.

"You know," Steve said after we were back in the car, "I think I'm going to take your friend Mako up on her offer, do the apartment-cat-sitting while she's gone."

"I thought you were allergic to cats."

"Actually, I've done pretty well with Mark's cat." He paused. "I feel like I have so much more energy—I think it's just that I'm more of a city person." I had noticed a difference in his walk. "I'll give you gals a break for a few days."

"Sure, makes sense. Of course."

Probable Causes for Spring in Steve's Step

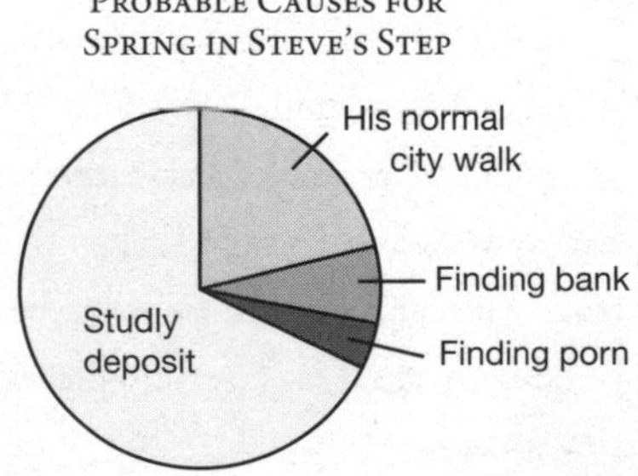

Three weeks is a long time to be a houseguest, or to have a houseguest, for that matter, and we still had three to go.

Steve went into the living room to call Bruce once we were home. He came back into the kitchen to make his pre-dinner tea and hang out while I was cooking. “Bruce invited me to the Cape after Christmas.” *The Cape's not the city.* I didn't say anything.

“You okay, honey?”

“Yeah, I guess I just thought . . . ” *Thought what? Thought you'd like living here? You'd want to help get ready for Christmas? You wouldn't become best friends with my best friend?*

“Look, it's a bit tricky . . . I'm trying to sort things out. I like working on my novel, but it's not like I have a deadline or anything. This is my vacation. And, you know, if everything works out, I've got to figure out how I'm going to do this once a year. I want to feel like something more than a visitor . . . ” He swallowed a sip of tea and the mug amplified his sigh.

“You're right,” I said. I stopped chopping. “Sorry.”

“What can I do to help?” He had his Enya CD poised above the CD drawer.

“Not that!” I said. He put on Emmylou Harris's *Wrecking Ball* and started doing the dishes.

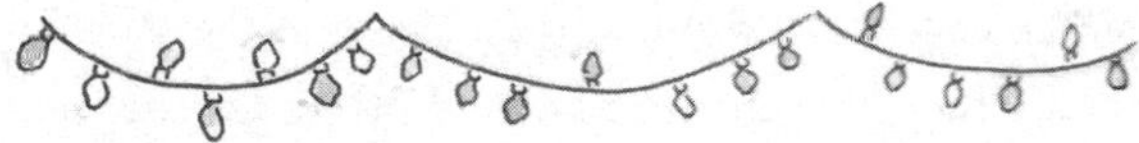

We were late for our third deposit. Steve was packing up for Mako's. It was the Friday before a Christmas Eve Monday, the height of the holiday ramp-up. “Another strange thing about this place,” I said in a low voice as we were getting off the elevator. “No holiday decorations.”

Steve shrugged. “Maybe it's out of respect—you know, the chemo, or the noncelebrants in the ‘family.’”

A new woman in a terry cloth turban and lab coat handled our intake. "Mrs. Baker?" *I'm sure you reserve your precision handling for the specimens.* "Mr. Dillon, right this way."

I kissed Steve good-bye. "Call me!"

There was a message from Steve on the home machine. The deposit had gone fine, but they had stuck him with more blood tests on his way out.

Truth was, there was hardly time to notice Steve was gone before it was time to pick him up at the train on Christmas Eve afternoon. I set him up with wrapping supplies in his room.

"Merry Christmas?" Lorene yelled up. I half expected to find her collapsed on the couch. She stood at the bottom of the stairs, draped in pine roping. "They gave me a really good price." Lorene had the roping wrapped in lights and hanging above the kitchen windows over the table by the time my mother and her dog arrived, followed by my older sister Robin and her dog, and my younger sister Meredith and her husband, Jonathan. Seven of us sat around the table and raised our glasses to a chorus of "Merry Christmas!" Lorene raised hers a second time: "To my new family!" *To Steve? Our baby plan?* It took several seconds to compute. She meant *my* family. It felt as if she'd been a part of it forever.

Steve's third deposit brought our total to thirty vials. I caught Mecke "in" on December 26th. A fourth deposit would kick us up to a higher storage fee. "You may want to consider it," Mecke suggested. "The values for your IUI specimens are above our minimums, but not by much. Perhaps we should have waited longer between collections, but Stephen is a mature donor and we all knew going into this . . . "

I was ovulating again. Maybe, by some miracle, we'd never need an intrauterine insemination; maybe we wouldn't need any of it. "I think we're done."

"All set, then. Let's see, his last deposit was December 21st, 2001. We can release this, provided we have Stephen's results, after June 21st, 2002." Steve would need to be retested for hep B, hep C, and HIV, which have a six-month incubation period.

My cycle was off. My period had been late after our first try. I wasted three ovulation predictor kits—I'd either missed my surge or never surged at all. We tried a couple more times before Steve went to the Cape, but I pinned less hope on the whole thing. Maybe that was good . . .

Egg SPECIAL NOTE: It is the largest (1/10 mm OR the size of a dot made by a sharp pencil) and only perfectly round cell in the human body.

We took Steve to Vermont for his last weekend. We showed him the place where we were going to have our wedding reception. It could have been that the end of the visit was near, or maybe we really had figured out how to live together. We read and wrote in front of the fireplace where Lorene and I would be married. Drank wine, played cards, and talked late into the night. The snow started falling our very last night, and we sent Steve outside.

We watched him from the kitchen windows; he was looking up, big flakes landing on his eyelashes, like a kid who had never seen snow.

GUEST BOOK

An Aussie in Vermont. Suzy tells me the house is 1700s. There isn't a building on my island that old. I love the rocking chairs and lamps, the comfy beds, the kitchen table and its memories, the warm generous feeling of the space. And, my first snow ever. Mountains of it . . .

I drove Steve to the airport the next day. The ride was quiet, just the two of us. We held hands. I didn't know how to thank him. I didn't know when I'd see him again. We entered the mouth of the tunnel that would dump us out at the airport, and Steve said, "This feels really strange. I'm kind of afraid to go home. Afraid I won't fit back in—not with Mark, I mean—with the life . . . "

I searched for something to say. "You've got the Australian Open coming up." We both love tennis. "That'll pull you in . . . You can come back. Anytime." We were pulling up to the curb. We barely had time to hug before Homeland Security shooed me away; Steve was still adjusting his backpack when I looked back in the rearview mirror.

He called the next day to say he was home. I didn't bother interrupting his life a week later to tell him I got my period. It was March when we heard from him next; he'd weathered a few severe withdrawal episodes, but he was comfortably reimmersed in his Australian life.

BEFORE I TURN 40 . . . I will learn to juggle

On May 28th, we met with our gynecologist. It was an 8:00 a.m. appointment. All the women in the waiting room were pregnant, shiny, and maternal without their coffee. My breasts shrank just looking at them.

The gynecologist scribbled notes while I updated her on our project: two unsuccessful at-home attempts, sperm in storage, sperm release coming up at the end of the month.

"Next month," Lorene reminded me. I forgot there were still a few days left in May.

She looked up. "I'm going to set you up for infertility treatment with Benjamin Rankin over at Boston IVF."

Infertility treatment? IVF? "But I thought everything—I thought you said the labs and everything were okay."

"They are." She leaned forward. "You're thirty-nine. You'll like Benjamin; I love him. He has been doing this for years. We could start you on Clomid, but I would rather you talk to Ben first."

"We can still try at home . . . "

"And we can still do your IUI here. It really doesn't change anything. We're trying to get you pregnant, right?" Lorene and I both nodded. "Schedule your appointment with Boston IVF, and call here when your OPK's positive at the end of—when's your sperm available?—end of June, and you'll come in, both of you if you want, for your insemination the next day."

WHAT ABOUT ALL THOSE WOMEN on TV???
Lynn Bezart Twins, Age 56
Liz Buttle, Age 60
Rosanna della Corte, Age 62

I spent the next couple of hours vetting Dr. Rankin—a very well-respected older gentleman, but not known for his comfort level working with people in "♀ur situati♀n." A friend of mine who'd had twins through IVF canvassed her friends and gave me another name that vetted out. His first available appointment was two months away. *Maybe we won't need it.* Lorene and I agreed to put the whole thing on dry ice until we got back from our honeymoon.

We exchanged our vows June 1st in front of the fireplace, our family, and just a few friends. There were little strawberries, champagne, and pictures afterward, and then, just married, we drove to the reception. The two of us walked through the empty restaurant to the terrace overlooking the garden, where all seventy-five guests erupted in applause and cheers. There were toasts and songs, dinner and dancing until after midnight. We have said to each other at least a hundred times since, "We got to have the wedding we always wanted."

Bottled June 1, 2002

Post-honeymoon, we were back on the insemination train. Timing-wise, everything was lining up: I was due to ovulate around the 28th; Steve's sperm would be released from quarantine June 22nd. But we ran into a problem. Only the director could authorize the release, and Tom Mecke wasn't returning my calls.

On July 1st, I took my ovulating self to the sperm bank, armed with Steve's HIV, hep B, and hep C test results. The Turban informed me that Steve's lab work was incomplete, and, furthermore, per the agreement I had signed, which she flashed at me, Steve's frozen sperm would be released only to a licensed physician. And, before I could ask, she announced that Tom Mecke was not on the premises—not behind the milky-blue doors, not watching videos in the collection room.

THIS is a hold-up! Gimme ALL the DILLON BAKER-BECKER sperm!

He returned my "call" nine days later. He was missing results for two tests, tests we'd discussed before Steve left in December. These tests weren't available in Australia and Tom had agreed to exempt us.

– 35	eggs per day
× **9**	days
– 315	eggs

"Tom"—I was too worn down to be angry—"I have already missed one cycle. I would be willing to assume the risk; is there something I can sign? Steve has been tested six ways from Sunday—"

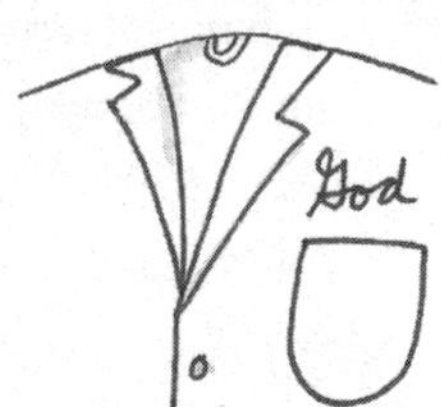

"Suzy, you can assume the risk for yourself, but I must protect the baby."

Steve's doctor found an offshore lab where she could overnight his blood, and we had the missing results a couple days before my next ovulation, which was shaping up to fall on the weekend.

Our gynecologist's practice, however, was not set up to accommodate weekend inseminations. Come September they would be able to refer weekend IUIs to the hospital, but that was neither here nor there, the nurse explained to Lorene. My doctor would not authorize an insemination until I repeated my Day 3 labs.

Lorene had had a few hours to get used to the idea by the time she told me. "Maybe it's all for the best; we go to Boston IVF next week." We had been so busy not getting pregnant, the appointment had snuck up on us.

The waiting room at Boston IVF was sleek, hushed, empty, actually. The dark carpeting, glossy light-wood furniture, and warm lights confirmed that you had entered the country's most experienced fertility center. And the fact that nobody else was in it wasn't the least bit off-putting; it wasn't a restaurant. Everyone was in their proper place, everything going according to plan. Within minutes we were escorted to our destination, and whoever came after us would find everything just as we had.

Dr. Penzias stood to shake our hands. He had an air of relaxed optimism that I sourced at the slight upturn of his nose and corners of his mouth. I wondered briefly why he (a bachelor somewhere between Lorene's age and mine) had chosen the field, but in terms of intimate information, these intakes are never an even exchange. The thank-you cards and baby photos on the hallway bulletin board were all I needed.

Within twenty minutes, we had a plan: three in-office inseminations, and if they (*not we*) were unsuccessful, Dr. Penzias would argue for a diagnosis of infertility (three short of the six inseminations required by most insurance companies) on the basis of a blocked right tube and my estrogen levels, which were good for my age, but my age, face it, was in the toilet. Then we would try hormones—follicle-stimulating hormone injections—and if we hadn't achieved pregnancy after three cycles with hormones, we agreed to discuss in vitro fertilization. It would have been rude not to agree to discuss IVF; it was Dr. Penzias's specialty, after all. The last point of the plan: We would have Steve's sperm transferred to the storage facility at Boston IVF ASAP.

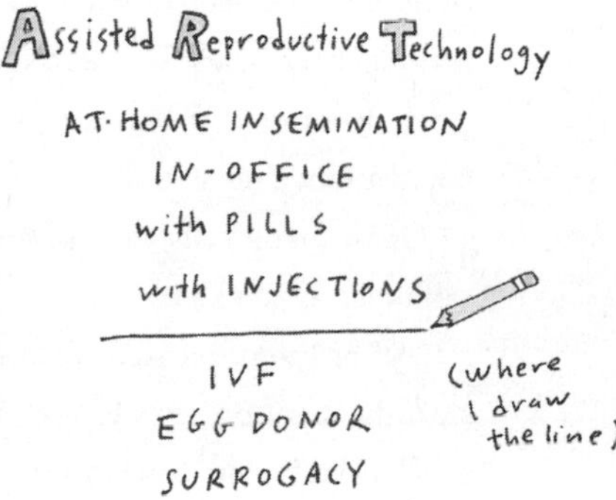

I immediately began conversations with Dr. Penzias's insurance liaison. An injectible hormone cycle would run us $2,000 to $3,000 out of pocket; however, Massachusetts has generous infertility coverage. The liaison had worked with several clients in "our situation," a.k.a. "women without exposure to sperm" in insurance circles. Since I was self-insured and at liberty to switch my coverage, she recommended a change. I would make the change after I got my Day 3 labs back, unless my Day 3 labs disqualified me. (GAME OVER!!!)

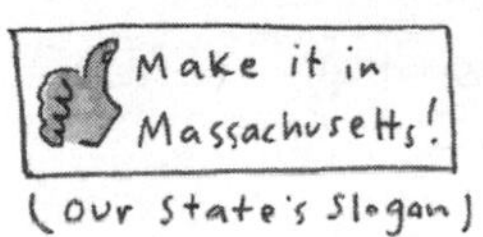

The lab results were on my answering machine. My follicle-stimulating hormone level had gone up from 8.8 to 10.4, but it was well below the cutoff. I switched my coverage, and while I was on a roll, I called Tom Mecke. Apparently, my communications alert had been downgraded. It was no longer necessary for me to speak with Tom; whomever I was speaking with could arrange my withdrawal.

"How many vials, and where are we sending them?"

"All of them, please. We're going to store them at Boston IVF, just easier . . ." as if I owed her an explanation.

I gave her the phone number for the andrology department, and the transfer was scheduled for August 29th. August 29th was a record hot day. I sat in front of the portable air conditioner in my studio, trying to unvisualize what was left of our microwaved sperm melting and pooling in the crevices of a taxi's backseat.

Andrology called to say our thirty vials had arrived safely. The end of a bad chapter. Finally.

If at First Second Third Fourth Fifth Sixth You Don't Succeed

We were coming up on Labor Day weekend, and I was getting ready to ovulate. Everything was in place for our OIOIUI (first official intra-office intra-uterine insemination): Boston IVF was open seven days a week, including Labor Day.

This time, the problem was me. I might be out of place, out of town; I'd bought tickets (my mother's and mine) to the U.S. Open months ahead of time, and we would be in New York the first half of the weekend. I packed up my OPK and went, intending to bomb back home if necessary.

Sine of Losing Mind

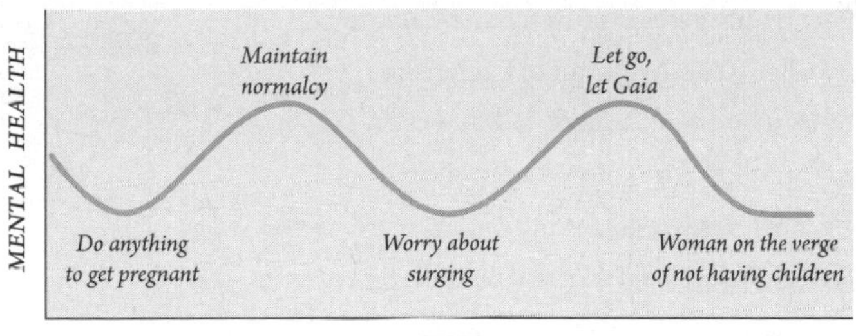

And, just in case I wasn't already worried enough about surging, Boston IVF called to tell Lorene that if I wasn't surging by Monday, I would need to come in for more blood work and an ultrasound.

I got the double-purple positive on my OPK at a rest area off Route 84 on our way home from New York. I practically skipped back to the car. *My first insemination, tomorrow*! There was a chance I'd eke out a conception in my thirties . . . I considered telling my mother, then thought better of it. She was what you might call *generally* supportive, not interested in the ins and outs, especially not the ins, of my project.

Inseminations took place two floors above Dr. Penzias's office at the fertility center. It seemed like a normal waiting room from the other side of the double glass doors. We entered and I announced myself at the desk: "Suzy Becker—"

"Suzy B.?" the receptionist gently corrected, running her pen under the privacy statement on the clipboard. "Sign in here." I signed in, and Lorene and I sat down below a poster that discouraged clients from bringing their children to their appointments, in deference to the difficulties other clients were experiencing conceiving. The sensitivity in the air was mildly oppressive.

"Michael R.? Heidi M.?" I looked. It was okay to look if someone was moving—taking a seat, selecting a new magazine, or getting up once their name was called. You just couldn't ogle the people who were seated. What was the beginning for us was the middle or end of a long road for others. *My infertility, if you want to call it that, is circumstantial, not biological.*

"Suzy B.?" Lorene and I both stood. We got lots of glances as people made their guesses.

Jackie, our inseminator, told us all about herself on our way down the hallway. She had switched from pediatrics to become an IVF nurse after her own experience with infertility, which resulted in a healthy baby girl. She was very proud of her client-success rate.

Since she was so free with her experience, I asked her about my one fear. "Does this feel like the tube test?"

"Oh, no, nothing like that," she assured me. "You know you can take Advil, right? I personally didn't. Remember, though, *only* Tylenol once there's a chance you're pregnant."

We entered the room and she closed the door. "All right! Before we get started, I need you to positively identify the sperm and sign this release." Jackie held up a test tube full of cloudy water with Steve's name on it.

Positively identify? Microscope, please! It didn't resemble any sperm I'd ever seen. I looked at Lorene and then signed. Jackie handed me a johnny. "Undress from the waist down." She turned her back to us, busying herself with the sperm. Then she turned around and patted the table. I laid down and put my feet in the stirrups.

Lorene held my hand. Jackie disappeared under the johnny, then bobbed back up. "Relax!" Lorene smiled. I breathed. *I am relaxed.* "Relax," Jackie said again. "Relax your butt muscles." The paper crinkled loudly as I dropped onto the table.

Jackie held up the empty syringe. "All done! Let's see—56 million sperm, 40% motile—there are 21 million sperm racing for that egg. The rate of progression is 3 out of 4, 4 is Olympic. Three is almost, in training."

I forgot all about the prescribed visualization.

The COLLECTIVE SHRIEK
(steve's sperm meet Suzy's egg)

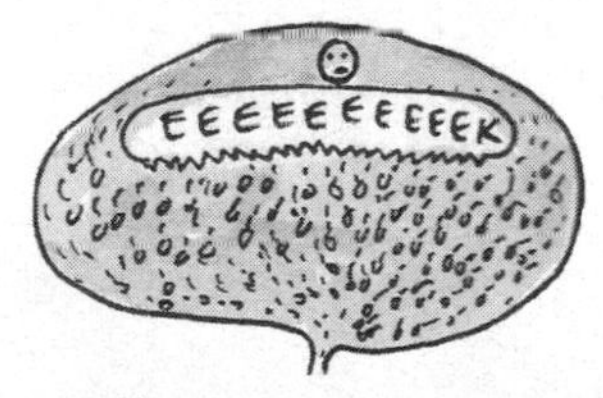

The 21 MILLION ABOUT-FACE!

"I may only have one tube—"

"One's all you need." She squeezed my toes. Lorene gave her a hug. "Lie there as long as you like, and take it easy the rest of the day. Schedule a pregnancy test for two weeks and call us if you have bleeding before."

Lorene drove us home. I maintained a pelvic tilt, my feet on the dashboard, until the ride was over. We had a whole sunny Sunday and Labor Day Monday ahead of us.

That afternoon we loaded Vita, Mister, and Mister's brother Hooley (ours for the weekend) into the back of the Subaru and went for an easy walk along the Nashua River. Five minutes from the parking lot, there was a loud cracking off to our left and we watched an old tree uproot and fall, slow motion, into the river. We stepped around the pile of sandy dirt where the roots had been and kept going.

ATTACK BEAVER

A quarter mile later, we heard an ominous growling sound. I picked up the pace (not even close to running), and we came upon Hooley. The two flat-coat retrievers had been swimming. Mister, at sixty-five pounds, was scurrying up and down the banks. Hooley, at a hundred pounds, had gotten himself stuck in the mudslide he'd made of the bank. I reached for his collar and pulled; the force of his coming unstuck catapulted me into the river.

"My body really didn't panic," I found myself explaining to Lorene as I was walking back to the car in my soaked clothes. "I was surprised, probably a little shocked by the coldness of the water, but . . . " I was not in zygote expulsion mode. Was I?

"Don't worry; besides, there's nothing we can do about it."

For the next two weeks, I tried to remind myself that people had remained pregnant under far more abusive circumstances.

I just wouldn't have been one of them. I got my period, done in by the Nashua River.

I turned forty in Vermont a few weeks later with Lorene, my sisters, Bruce, and the dogs. It felt like putting a period (not that kind) on the end of my thirties. I was happy to have the brain surgery and dating behind me. I had a feeling of fullness—love, stability, contentment—that kind. So I didn't get pregnant in my thirties. Forty is only a couple months' difference.

WHY MEDICALLY SUPERVISED IUIs ARE BETTER THAN SEX

1. EVERYBODY'S UP FOR a QUICKY.
2. NO ONE HAS TO GET EXCITED.
3. YOU CAN KEEP YOUR SOCKS ON.
4. SOMEONE ELSE CLEANS the SHEETS.

We tried again in October. My brother called halfway through the waiting cycle for my belated birthday. "I wish I could help, Sue-Sue. I have to be careful—I sneeze on someone and they're pregnant."

"You're supposed to sneeze into your elbow now." I was feeling optimistic at that moment; my boobs were swollen.

Pseudocyesis
Sympathetic* or *False Pregnancy

The erroneous notion of carrying a baby. An individual experiences all prevalent symptoms, except for presence of fetus.

Documented in:

- females bearing strong desire to conceive
- male partners of pregnant women (also known as *couvade*)
- dogs, pandas, and other animals

Five days later, I got my period. This time there was no one, no incident, nothing else to blame. I looked at myself in the mirror.

I decided to grow my hair out, go for something more maternal. Lump the awkward-hair stage and the no-exercise-writing-a-book-butt stages together. I called Lorene to tell her my news—period and hair—and went back up to work.

An hour later, my sister Meredith let herself in the kitchen door. She called up, "Bad timing?"

I came down. "No . . . or yes. I just got my period." She hugged me. "Ow! My boobs!" I held on to her and cried. "I'm sorry. I didn't realize I was this upset. Did you have a meeting out here or— ?"

"This is bad timing," she said. All of a sudden, I knew. "I'm pregnant."

I'd imagined the scene at least a hundred times, except I was pregnant, too. "Oh my gahh!" I hugged her again. I *was* happy for her. "Wow, I didn't know, you didn't tell me you were trying." We were so busy talking about my trying.

"We weren't really, I mean, we were getting ready to. I was sure it was going to take forever," she paused. "The baby is due on Dad's birthday."

I could never match that. "Want some coffee, no, wait, you can't drink coffee, tea? Water?" She had to go; she just wanted me to be the first (after Jonathan) to know.

I went back up to my studio, as if I could work again, and cried some more. Everyone was getting pregnant—my doctor, my friend Michaela, my sister . . . *Why does it have to be so hard for me?*

Think about why:

(1) You're 40, (2) You're a lesbian,

(3) You've tried FIVE times not FIVE YEARS.

Have you chugged cough syrup?
Spent $30K?

Plastered your ying yang with egg whites?

> **Things could be worse . . .**
>
> It took Japan's Crown Princess Masako eight years to get pregnant and then she gave birth to a girl, which was considered a failure. (Her imperial duty was to produce a male heir.)

I went back to work, looking forward to the glass of wine Meredith would not be having with her dinner.

In December, after our third try failed, we had another meeting with Dr. Penzias—the why-it-isn't-working meeting. "Call it system design, or error: eighty percent of the time, between healthy, fertile couples in their reproductive prime, it doesn't work. Simple as that." *Nature's contraception.* "Your age is a factor, we've got a possible tube issue—but we want to do better. We *can* do better. I'm going to write a letter to your insurance company and see if we can get that infertility diagnosis. We could start the hormones this month."

We couldn't. And I was disappointed. Now I *wanted* the infertility diagnosis; like the gynecologist had said, "It doesn't change anything." We want to get me pregnant.

"What about the two tries at home?" I asked the insurance liaison, the bearer of bad news.

"You can take it up with them yourself, but I'll tell you ahead of time, even if you had documentation—they rejected one of our client's claims. She had all of her sperm-bank receipts. They said it had to be an in-office, 'medically supervised' procedure. She yelled at them, 'What do you think I'm doing, drinking it?' They didn't budge."

We had Jackie the inseminator again for our fourth try. She was wearing a Santa cap but there was no ho-ho-ho to go with it. I was a success-rate spoiler. She looked at our paperwork, then she looked at us. "Why are you using just the one vial? Most people do two, at least two."

"They do? Can we? Let's!" we said. We weren't buying it by the vial; it made complete sense. Steve had deposited ten at a whack. *Why didn't you mention it the first time?*

"I can't, it's too late for this insemination. Something to keep in mind for the next time." She'd already written this time off.

We minimized our table time; Lorene had to get back for work. We assumed our positions in the car—Lorene at the wheel, my feet on the dash—and rolled out of the garage. Lorene wondered out loud, "What else don't we know?"

She dropped herself at the shop; I drove home. The house looked beautiful. Lorene had already hung the Christmas greens. The tree (Lorene's pick) was smaller and fatter than in years past, and fuller than ever with decorations. We wouldn't have had room for the stork ornament I bought back in November. I'd given it to Meredith; *I could always buy another one for us.*

I had less holiday stuff left to do than usual, but I still could've used another week, just to get in the spirit. I was dealing with the cumulative effects of four months without exercise, without getting pregnant, and I was no better at retail widowhood the second time around.

Next Christmas, the brain book would be in the bag. The baby question would be answered. It would be Meredith's baby's first Christmas. Next Christmas, I promised myself, we'd have a Christmas.

NEW
LOVE
5/01 - 12/02

MOURNING
the WAY WE USED TO:
look at each other,
be kind to each other.
make love to each other.
have all the time in
the world for each other.

I recorded these things as if by identifying them, I might, at some future date, be able to retrieve them. Lorene and Vita were sleeping crown to crown, sharing a pillow on the couch in the Christmas-tree firelight. I squished myself in next to the two of them. *This is enough. We are enough.*

With the holidays behind us, I went into work overdrive. The brain book was due mid-February, and I needed to do a chapter's worth of finished art (twenty spot illustrations) daily to stay on schedule. The work endorphins gave my psyche a lift. At chapter three, I got my period; I didn't bother to tell Lorene until she got home.

> **From:** Steve
> **Subject:** Thinking of you
> **Date:** January 3, 2003
>
> Hi Honey, What's happening? I realize this has to be ten times harder for you. The trick is to see the humour, though it's not always easy. Sometimes I worry we won't be friends if there is no baby. (No pressure!) If you want to debrief or if you feel like a chat, I could ring on Thursday or Friday.
> Big cuddles to you, Lorene and even those funny dogs, Steve

We had to cut our Martin Luther King getaway weekend short to do our insemination. Meredith and Jonathan, and Lucy and Jim, the proprietors of the Burlington B&B, gave us a seven o'clock send-off in the snowy circular driveway that Sunday morning. We intended to be back by late afternoon: Lorene would drive and I'd do my reverse shotgun—but we lost steam.

We had requested three vials for our fifth try. Before our inseminator let them fly, she observed that their rate of progression was neither, to borrow Jackie's terms, "Olympic" nor "in training." At a rate of two, they probably cut gym. "Next time," she advised us, "you should request a minimum rate of three." Lorene and I looked at each other. Still, it *was* twenty-seven million sperm, and we only needed one . . .

This time I called Dr. Penzias's nurse and asked her, "What else don't we know?" She suggested we come in and pose the question to Dr. Penzias. He found it "interesting" that we'd been told we could increase our chances by using more sperm, and certainly a higher rate of progression was desirable, but common sense—a layperson's intuition—didn't really apply here. There is little evidence to support the claim that either piece of unauthorized advice significantly improved our chances of getting pregnant.

He reviewed our plan. "If you aren't pregnant, which you may well be," he smiled, "we have one more IUI. And if that's not successful, which it may well be, then we can begin the hormones."

That night, Lorene and I watched *ER*. I'd started watching in 1995, during my days teaching in a charter school, when it was relaxing to watch people doing a job that was more stressful than mine. Lorene and I had watched Kerry, the lesbian head of the *ER*, inject herself with hormones before undergoing IVF (off camera). Last week, she'd miscarried. This week, her partner was giving her a consulation gift. Kerry snapped, "This is to be expected! Thirty percent of IVFs end in miscarriage." I blanked out the next couple of scenes.

"Wait, what was it, only fifteen percent of IVFs work, and then thirty percent of those end in miscarriage?"

The Math
(miscarry the one...)
15% – 30% 10.5%

"We're not going to do IVF," Lorene said, and kissed my knee.

When our January attempt failed, our February IUI morphed into one last thing we had to do before we could get started with hormones in March.

A week after the insemination, Lorene had made a fire in our bedroom fireplace. She'd kept it going for two full days; the room had never been so warm. It was hard to think about taking the dogs out in the morning. We lay in bed talking over their barking. "I've been thinking," she said. "We can't go to California in April. What if you're pregnant?" *Or, what if the dogs quit barking and brought us breakfast in bed?*

"What if I'm *not* pregnant? We'll just miss a month of trying." We were supposed to meet my friends in Joshua Tree; it was their wedding present to us.

"I'm just worried about taking the time off now; after we have the baby, I'm going to need lots of time off and—"

"I'll take maternity leave, you won't have to—"

"But I'll want to." *She seriously thinks I'm going to get pregnant.*

"I think I really need the trip," I said. "Don't worry."
It'll never happen. "It'll work out."

Instant Convert

Dr. Penzias made the doctor issue of *Boston* magazine. "Look, he's cute as a bug's ear," Lorene said. I looked again, more for a point of self-comparison.

LORENE'S DEFINITION of "CUTE"

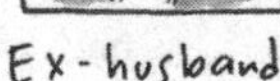

We congratulated him at our March appointment. My pregnancy test was negative, although I hadn't gotten my period yet. We re-re-reviewed what he liked to call our options, which were indistinguishable from our plan, since there was really only one—the follicle-stimulating hormone (FSH) injections. I was supposed to drink lots of water and call in on the first day of my new cycle. The injections would start on Day 3. We could stop downstairs for a patient-information session on our way out, or we could come back at our convenience. We went for the latter, just in case I never got my period. Besides, *ER* had given us a pretty good introduction.

Day 1, I called the nurse to schedule the info session and I spoke with the pharmacy. We needed a Saturday-with-nobody-at-home delivery. The nobody-home part wasn't a problem, but the below-freezing temperatures complicated things. I had to hang up to think about which of my neighbors I wanted to bring into the loop, then I remembered, we had Lorene's shop.

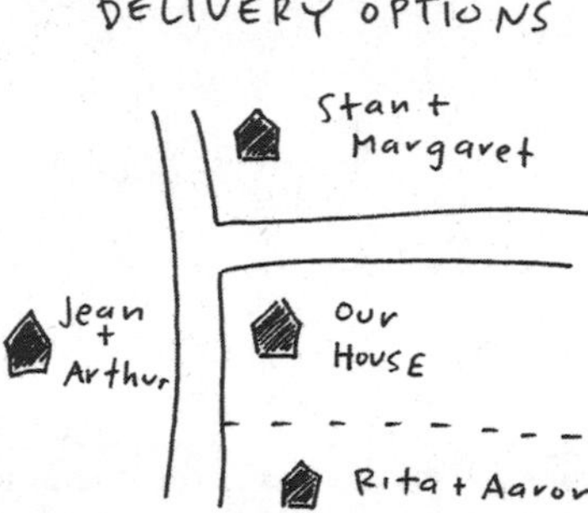

Lorene printed out the website's injection instructions and read them out loud as we drove in for our information session. We sat down at a long table, just the two of us. We *were* the information session.

The injection itself turned out to be the least of our worries. First, the hormone powder had to be mixed with sterile water. Then everything had to be sterilely transferred from one tiny glass ampule to another, using needles and syringes.

Lorene practiced the injection in a rubber cork. "That's all there is to it," the nurse said, smiling a Friday-four-p.m. smile and disposing of the syringe in the biohazardous waste box. "Do you want to try again?"

INSEMINATIONS have to be MEDICALLY-SUPERVISED but INJECTIONS don't?

I looked at Lorene. The nurse added, "It's all written down. There's a video on the website, and you can call the on-call doctor at any point in the process . . . "

Lorene said, "I'll try it again." I felt myself relax.

"Have you ordered your FSH?" the nurse asked me while Lorene was mixing the fake stuff.

I launched into our delivery dilemma as I was signing her orientation attendance. "The pharmacy's right in this building, you know, you could just pick it up."

The pharmacist handed us our shopping bag: the FSH, sterile water, syringes, needle/biohazardous-waste "sharps" box, a purse-size cold-pack carrier (free gift from the makers of Gonal-f FSH), and I threw in my Cow Tale that I'd purchased from their small candy selection.

Sunday night, we headed upstairs around 9:30. We planned to retire with the paper after our first injection. Lorene laid out the written instructions, the ampules of FSH and distilled water, and the syringe on the windowsill. She calmly mixed the FSH and drew it up with the syringe. I lay on the rug. She knelt down and leaned toward me. Misplacing the intimacy of the moment, I thought she was going to kiss me. Instead, she lifted my shirt and rubbed my belly with an alcohol wipe. "Yow! Cold!" I complained.

"Baby!" she laughed and reached for the syringe. "Okay." She uncapped the needle, pinched my belly skin, and announced, "On the count of three, you're going to feel a sharp prick. One, two . . . okay.

Okay, just a second." She looked at the tip of the needle over the tops of her glasses. "All right. Ready? Okay, one, two . . . " She looked at me. "Do *you* want to do this?"

Me? I couldn't get my finger to stay put when we had to do the finger-prick blood test in high school biology. "All you."

"I hate needles. Hold on a minute." She took a deep breath. "Okay, this is not going to give you cancer." She started over with the skin pinch. "Here we go. One, two, three." Done.

"Thank you."

"You're nice to say that," she said.

"No, I'm really grateful. I'm so glad I'm *not* doing this alone."

She lay down on top of me, then pushed herself up suddenly. "Oh, God, does it hurt?"

"Not a bit." She went downstairs and poured herself a whiskey.

Cancer Court 2020

Judge: Your wife was concerned. How about you? Did **YOU** ever think about what she was injecting?

Me: Like what was in it? Mouse pee or hamster hormones or something? At that point, it seemed like our only option. And I trusted Dr. Penzias . . . a doctor wouldn't let you harm yourself. *(Courtroom laughter)*

Judge: Order! (*Laughter dies down)*

Judge: Was **NOT** getting pregnant an option?

We kept up our 9:30 nightly; we got the one-two-threes down to two. On Friday morning, we incorporated the blood work and ultrasound monitoring into our early-morning routine. The two of us would flop into the car, no shower, no breakfast; the inconvenience never even had a chance to register in our uncaffeinated state.

I was just starting to wake up when I was in the ultrasound room. The technician provided live commentary on my follicles. "One on the left ovary, lots of good-sized ones coming along. None on the right, a handful of up-and comers."

"What's a good-sized-one?"

"We like to see them larger than twelve millimeters."

We received our updated injection instructions by phone that afternoon: Stay the course. More monitoring on Sunday.

I had a hard time differentiating the effects of the hormones from other inputs, like the added stress I experience working on a new job. My first cartoon for *Seed* magazine was due in a week. I'd submitted three sketches and hadn't heard anything, so I Gonal-e-mailed the editor. She called the next day to say she liked all three, and she'd decided on one, with one small

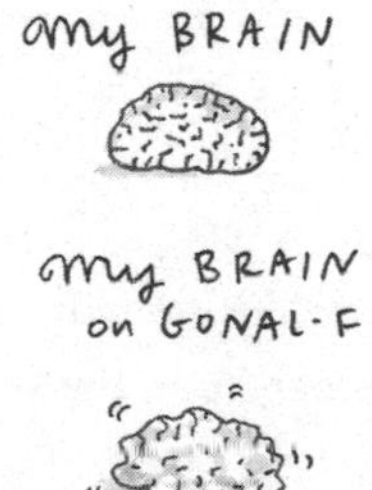

change: "Can you make the scientist look less like a stereotypical scientist? We're trying to make science sexy here."

INTRODUCING

Let me tell you what we're trying to do around here—graphic shorthand!

HORMONAL ME

"You want a hubba scientist?"

"Yes," she laughed. I drank a big glass of water, gave him a new head, and faxed it off.

I actually felt the effects of hydration—going from zero (not counting coffee or lettuce) to sixty-four ounces—more profoundly than the hormones. After a lifetime of proud public-bathroom avoidance, I was reduced to making pit stops on my way into Boston.

Q: How do you get so much done?
A: I don't go to the bathroom.

TIME spent thinking about when/where to go
+ TIME spent going
+ TIME spent getting back to work
= TIME not spent working

On Sunday (Day 10), left ovary was ahead. We went to Meredith and Jonathan's for dinner carrying a cake tin full of injection paraphernalia. The extra bottles we needed to mix a new batch of Gonal-f wouldn't fit in the free purse-size carrier. Lorene also believed we should be bringing dinner for, not accepting dinner from, the six-months-pregnant people. I promised I would make them dinner if we were ever lucky enough to be in that boat.

After we did the dishes, Meredith got on her computer in the living room and Jonathan went up to clean out the litter box, leaving us the privacy of the kitchen. Lorene opened the cake tin. "Shit!" We'd brought all of the equipment and none of the instructions. "Never mind, I think I remember," she said. She filled the syringe full of sterile water and inserted it into the Gonal-f bottle. "Nothing's coming out . . . Nothing's coming out. There's too much pressure, NOTHING'S COMING OUT!"

"Try pulling the plunger back." She did and the sterile water squirted all over.

"Shit! Look, it *was* going in! I should've never listened to you."

I shot back, "Don't blame me, I thought you were asking for help."

Lorene lowered her voice and said, "I don't want to have this conversation in front of other people," just as Meredith walked in. I laughed at the timing. "Don't laugh at me!" Lorene said. She slammed her keys on the floor and left the house.

Meredith helped me put everything back into the cake tin. Lorene and I drove home in silence. A few miles from home, I managed an "I'm sorry."

> When we are angry, our tendency is to punish the other person, but when we do, there is only an escalation of the suffering. Instead send a gift. Offer what is needed.
>
> —Thich Nhat Hanh

"I'm sorry, too." She was sobbing, sorrier than I was, as if it was all her fault.

We found another bottle of sterile water in the kit at home. Lorene took her time (we were already late) and mixed up the new batch. The shot hurt; we had run out of new spots.

"Thank you," I said, and went to my studio to work. Lorene went to sleep.

The next morning, we dragged ourselves out of bed for another ultrasound. There was no real reason for Lorene to come with me, but there was never any question, even after a bad night, that she would. We were in this together.

Right ovary had tied up the score. Updated instructions: One more dose of Gonal-f, then Pregnyl, the ovulation-stimulating hormone, the next night.

We were in the chute: IUI Thursday. A pressure in my lower abdomen, something like having to go to the bathroom, had been building.

LORENE

I've known her forever

I don't know her at all

She does this sometimes

She's gone off the deep end.

Lorene went back to bed when we got home. She was still in bed at dinnertime.

I made her come down to eat and she went back up as soon as we finished. The next morning she woke up, got out of bed, showered, and got dressed as if she hadn't stayed in bed all day the day before, and there was no further mention made of it.

Thursday's IUI, two vials, was routine. My ovaries had deflated and the red Pregnyl needle patch was gone by Friday. I harbored a hope that *this* was the cycle; Lorene must have, too, but the hope was too tired to mention.

I woke up with my period on the first of April. I lay quietly in bed waiting for Lorene to wake up so I could tell her. "Is this an April Fools' joke?" *Ba-dum-bum.*

We skipped April; we had the trip to California. Lorene and I spent two days in Hope Springs at a desert motel that had been converted to a laid-back spa. I watched her float on a blue raft in the hottest pool, my breasts (which still insisted I was pregnant) spilling out of the top of my bathing suit.

I was determined not to feel disappointed in Hope Springs. I felt at peace, the wind riffling through the palm trees. The landscape was so unfamiliar, it did not invite the ruminations on relocation that could undercut the peace of vacationing in a place closer to home. I had a pile of good books, CDs, my wife, and we were going to see our friends the next day . . . I wasn't wanting for anything, no excepts.

Jane and David met us outside of Joshua Tree at a wonderfully funky inn. They'd driven down from Berkeley. After drinks and dinner, we went back to our own adobe casitas. I gave Lorene the lamp side of the bed and fell asleep on my back in minutes. A couple hours later, I awoke in the same position, staring up at the ceiling, my head buzzing long enough for me to recall the feeling, and then I had a seizure. Just a small one. The first one I'd had since my surgery four years earlier.

There were the snuffly breaths after it was over, then the thick tongue. Lorene was sitting up on her elbows observing me. "Your right hand was waving, your elbow bent—the bed was shaking."

It was a few minutes before I could talk. "It's not supposed to happen." This is the one goddamn surgical benefit I was promised.

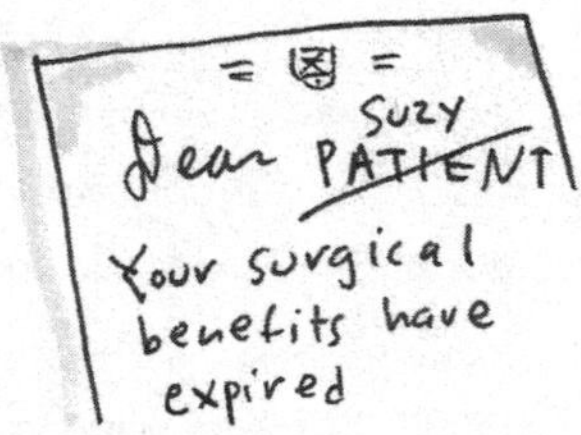

"It scares me. I don't want you trying to get pregnant again until we know."

"Until we know what?"

"Why you had a seizure. I don't want you giving birth—" She was crying. "I don't want to lose you."

I held her. I had been told that thirty percent of the time, seizures are of "unspecified origin." Neurologists cannot determine what causes them after months or years of ruling out every god-awful neurological disease on the books. I didn't have time. "We'll call Dr. Finn when we get back." *Maybe something was different. Maybe it's why I can't get pregnant.* I flipped the TV on and watched, dozing off and on, until the sun came up.

Dr. Finn, my neurosurgeon, wasn't the least bit concerned about my seizure. As his nurse explained, "Seizures will be your Achilles' heel—the warning signal you need to slow down and rest." *On vacation? And what were they before the brain surgery? Never mind.*

The seizure seemed a long time ago, or California is a long ways away, anyway; Lorene and I resumed our lives, went back to trying to get pregnant, planning Meredith's baby shower and another bike-a-thon.

The brain book made the cover of Workman Publishing's spring catalog. A promising development, it seemed, until I heard from the head of chain-store sales, "Suzy, I'll be honest with you, I don't get the book . . .

I don't get it either!

I was wondering if you would come down and have lunch with me."

I accepted his invitation. Less than five minutes later, *ping!* I (and a long list of *Who's Who* at Workman) received his e-mail:

> **From:** Jim
> **Subject:** Lunch and Presentation by Cover Girl Suzy Becker
> **Date:** May 15, 2003
>
> Suzy Becker will share her new book with us on May 22nd at 1:00 p.m.
> Lunch will be served. Please RSVP!
> Thanks, Jim

Presentation? Now I would have to cram making slides into the next day's schedule, which began with an 8:00 a.m. appointment at Boston IVF and concluded with an 8:30 p.m. Board of Selectmen's meeting, followed by my 9:30 shot.

It was after 9:30 when I raced up my studio stairs to get the updated instructions for our nightly shot.

> MESSAGE #1:
>
> "Your ovaries are responding very well to the hormones. With your permission, we'd like to convert the cycle from an IUI to an IVF. Otherwise, we'll need to scrap this cycle. Please call back before five."
>
> MESSAGE #2:
>
> "Please continue the Gonal-f at 187 to keep our options open. You are scheduled for more blood work at 7:45 tomorrow morning, and we will confer again tomorrow afternoon."

"IVF?" Lorene squawked. I had repeated the message in my most matter-of-fact tone.

"It doesn't matter. We'll just do the 187 and find out all about it tomorrow."

"You don't want to do IVF," she reminded me.

"You don't want to scrap the cycle . . . " Lorene got in bed with her laptop, and I went back to my studio to make slides.

The next afternoon, I was home to receive the call. Instead of three or four follicles, I had busted out fourteen. Now I had to decide (they had less than an hour to get approval from my insurance) whether I wanted to do IVF or scrap the cycle.

Knowing nothing about IVF, I should've had a hundred questions. I came up with one: "Will I be able to resume IUIs next cycle?" *Like normal infertile people?* The answer was yes. If I gave my approval, my "egg retrieval" would be scheduled for Monday, the transfer for Thursday. *Cover Girl Presentation Day!*

DOLLY

Was Dolly an IVF baby?

I called Lorene. Neither one of us could have imagined choosing IVF until it was pitted against scrapping the cycle. There was no discussion. "Go for it!" Lorene said.

I called my editor. No answer. I called the patient coordinator back: "What about a Friday transfer?" *An extra day in the test tube, petri dish, or whatever.* Not possible.

The editor called back and I briefed her on my baby project. "Are you crazy? Go for it! The book can wait!"

Yes!

She is the World's Best Editor.

She doesn't give a fat rat's ass about your book.

I dialed the patient coordinator with forty-eight minutes to go. "I'll do it."

"We're on!" she was feeling the excitement. "Wait! We didn't give you an anti-ovulatory—we're on, as long as you don't ovulate between now and then."

"Can you give it to me now?"

"Can you get to the pharmacy before 5:30?" I was in the car at 4:32. Sitting in rush hour traffic a few miles from the pharmacy at 5:40. I ran in at 6:10, still hoping. There was a note: My prescription had been called in to the other branch, which was open until 7:00. At 7:15, I was back home, anti-ovulatory in hand.

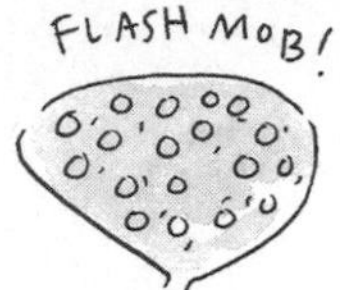

Saturday's blood work confirmed I hadn't ovulated. And the technician was thrilled with my follicles—eighteen at least.

We spent the rest of the day getting ready for Meredith's surprise shower—cooking, wrapping presents, cleaning and decorating the house, preparing the pin-the-hair-on-the-bald-baby-Meredith's-head game.

Meredith arrived Sunday morning dressed for a day of driving, double-checking the Ride FAR route. She was one month away from her due date. She was telling me a story as we walked toward the living room, "We stopped at Starbucks on the way over. A complete stranger asked me if I was going to 'have a vaginal birth'!"

"Did you say nasal?" I opened the living room door.

"SURPRISE!"

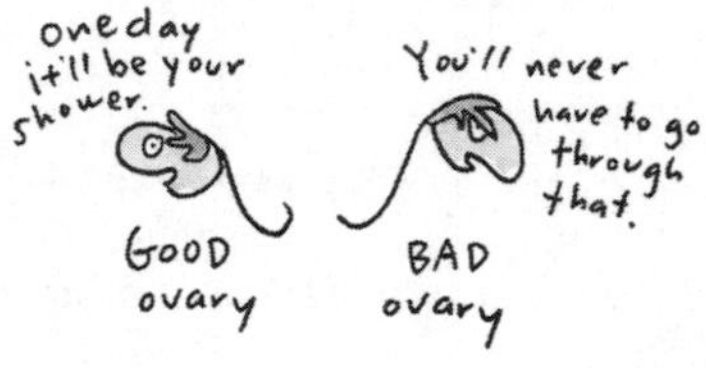

We were all exhausted by the end of the shower. Lorene and I napped in the hammock, then I got up to complete Workman's publicity questionnaire, the consolation prize I planned to attach to my lunch cancellation notice. I hit "send" and immediately worried my efforts to provide sales hooks for the book were sinking it further.

I printed out the pre-op forms and admission information so I could take it all to bed. A nurse had called in the middle of Meredith's shower to confirm my retrieval and to remind me to arrive preregistered.

Lorene and I had finished reading the ten-page consent form and signed at eleven, one hour before my fluids cutoff. "I don't think I've ever been under general anesthesia before . . . maybe once, for my wisdom teeth."

"Are you worried?"

"Should I be? I guess the aftereffects are worse, right?" That had been a selling point for my "awake" brain surgery. "I'm used to being awake . . . It's weird, don't you think, that we don't know who the surgeon is until we walk in?"

"Mmm. Are you afraid?"

"No." I got myself one last glass of water and we worked on the crossword puzzle until we turned out the lights.

There wasn't much incentive to get out of bed the next morning. No coffee, no breakfast, nowhere to be until ten. "C'mon," Lorene prodded me, "it's trash day." I rolled out of bed, did the trash, showered, and went up to my office to collect a few things I could do while I was resting post-retrieval.

Dr. Rankin (the gynecologist's referral we'd dissed) was our surgeon. The nurse described him as more "laid-back" than Dr. Penzias. Dr. Penzias had never struck us as uptight, but we weren't nurses. Dr. Rankin was very kind, not the least bit disapproving, but Lorene never passed up an opportunity to make an extra-good impression. She complimented his accent, which he revealed was Scottish.

The anesthesiologist arrived and Lorene kissed me good-bye, gave my wedding ring-less hand a last squeeze, and went off to the waiting room. The next thing I remember, I was being transferred to the post-op area. Lorene came in about the same time as the saltines and ginger ale. We were free to go, or to stay as long as we liked. The lab would call us with the official egg count in the afternoon.

Egg Retrieval

The doctor uses a vaginal ultrasound to guide a hollow needle to the ovaries. The needle punctures the follicle and the egg and fluid are suctioned out.

The count was twenty. (The average count is ten to twelve.) I called to brag to my IVF-vet friend. She was unimpressed. (She was also alone with her twins, without child care for the week.)

"The egg count is unreliable," she said. "What really matters is how many fertilize."

She was always one step ahead. Lorene's and my sanity-preservation plan required us to celebrate the step we were on. I stayed in bed, did a little work. I felt fine, felt like I was slacking, in fact, since I felt no pain, just my normal afternoon drowsiness. I closed my eyes for a second and woke up two hours later when the phone rang.

"Suzy, it's Margaret" (the neighbor from across the street), "Do you have any eggs?" *Do I have any eggs? Do* I *have any eggs? Well, Margaret, let me tell you. I have TWENTY! TWENTY EGGS!* "I just need one."

She was at the door a few minutes later. I handed her the lone egg, recognizing, after the fact, that my bedhead conveyed a certain not-exactly-working-from-home ethic.

Fourteen of my twenty eggs fertilized. I called my IVF friend. She was not impressed. "What really matters is how many good embryos you get."

We got two "beautiful eight-cell embryos" and one six-cell embryo which we agreed to freeze.

The transfer doctor's resemblance to Al Franken stuck with me, whereas his last name, something one-syllable, did not. He put the two beautiful embryos back into my uterus (while I was off in general-anesthesia land), and we were back on the road an hour later. Dr. Franken called around noon to report that my six-cell embryo never made it into the freezer; it had started to fragment. *So much for my two beauties.*

I couldn't refrain from asking, while trying to head off a nonanswer, "I know you may not know, and your answer won't change anything, I'll still have to wait to see whether I get pregnant, and of course, I won't hold you to it, I'm just asking, really for my, you know, my peace of mind, what's the likelihood of the transfers fragmenting?"

"As you said. We don't know."

The IVF coordinator called in the late afternoon. She was following up: Fourteen out of twenty was a high fertilization rate, very promising. Two embryos out of fourteen fertilized eggs was very low. The results of the stain testing they'd done on the extra eggs and sperm might tell Dr. Penzias something about the egg/sperm quality, which could inform the next cycle.

I interrupted. "So this one's not going to work out?"

"I'm sorry, I didn't mean to suggest that. Not at all. You only need one good egg."

It's just that that one can be so damn hard to come by.

A Little Bit Pregnant

It was a rainy spring. The rain took the pressure off weekend yard work, although some of the pressure wended its way into the weekday evenings. The sounds of our neighbors' mowers marred the few good sunsets we might have otherwise enjoyed.

TIPS TO STAY SANE WHILE WAITING FOR YOUR PREGNANCY TEST RESULTS

1. Once your transfer has taken place, there is nothing you can do to influence the outcome. Pessimism, anxiety, etc. will not influence outcome.
2. Embryos cannot fall out (into a pothole, toilet, etc.).
3. Progesterone will cause confusing symptoms. Only a test will tell if you are pregnant.

Lorene and I had gone to Vermont to celebrate our first anniversary, leaving the yard and house far behind. Sunday morning, the actual day, we went to Dot's Diner, where we'd had our first "civilly united"

breakfast. We brought the *New York Times* back to the house and read all through the afternoon in front of a fire. There were long stretches that weekend when I didn't care if I was pregnant. We would have a happy, more self-indulgent life together without children.

Then I started to bleed. I cried for a few minutes alone in the bathroom. Lorene looked up when I walked back in. "I'm sorry," I said. She needed no further explanation. "I really thought *this* time . . . "

"I know," she said. She was crying, too.

The rest of the day, the sight of red—cutting cherries, red sock fuzz on the white porcelain bathtub—would turn my stomach. And then the bleeding stopped, and I started having cramps.

"You know," Lorene said, "spotting and cramps are pregnancy symptoms." By the time we dined on bread, cheese, baby artichokes, and defrosted wedding cake, I was willing to believe again that I could be pregnant. Spotting and cramping certainly marked a departure from the first seven failed attempts.

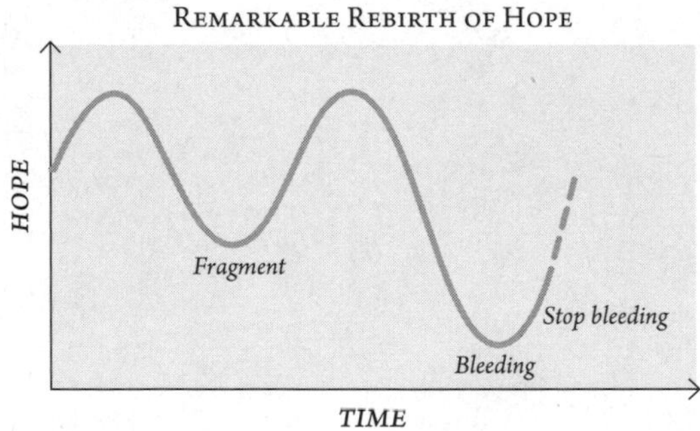

The sun was out on Tuesday, the morning of the pregnancy test. Lorene was now positive I was pregnant. I had gone so far as to think maybe I might be, too. Getting to take the blood test was, itself, something of a milestone.

An hour and a half after I had been back at work, pretending to have a normal day, my studio phone rang. Lorene appeared on my stairs out of nowhere. It was Boston IVF. It did occur to me in that split second that ten thirty (vs. after lunch or at the end of the day) was an auspicious time for a call, and I wasn't all wrong.

"Suzy, your pregnancy test was positive," the nurse said flatly. I gave Lorene the thumbs-up and she gasped. "However, the positive hCG value is low," which would explain the nurse's affect. "There is a fifty percent chance of a healthy pregnancy. We'd like you to come back in for another test in two or three days."

Lorene and I sat on the stairs and I repeated the nurse's four sentences. Three days was more convenient, but we didn't want to wait. (And since when was convenience a factor?)

Human Chorionic Gonadotrophin (hCG)
A hormone produced by the developing placenta post-conception, measurable in blood or urine.

After I scheduled the test, I succumbed to an online hCG-research session while my cartoons, book, Ride FAR, and the library roof grant application waited. Best-case scenario: delayed implantation. Probable-case scenario: miscarriage or ectopic pregnancy.

That night, I started to bleed heavily. I would've just thought it was my period if I hadn't had that stupid pregnancy test. We were sorry all over again. Lorene wanted to cancel our dinner plans to stay home and cry. I couldn't be convinced of the upsides. *THIS has already taken up too much of our emotional energy.* Besides, if I started crying, I might never stop.

My hCG value, with brazen disregard for my heavy bleeding, doubled on Thursday, which was a "good" sign. My healthy-pregnancy odds stayed at fifty percent. In just two short days, these sounded like "good" odds to me. The nurse suggested I curtail all physical activity: "We're going to treat this as a pregnancy with a bleed."

Meanwhile, I had to treat it as a seventh-grade menstrual period. No tampons. Nothing up my ying-yang other than the progesterone suppository, which was helping me hold at fifty percent. I had a supersize self-stick sanitary napkin stuck between my legs.

Meredith woke us up the next morning. Two weeks ahead of her due date, her water had broken. I padded up my pants, packed up my gear, and got the phone chain going. I gave my dad's partner, Linda, the news first, then I paused the chain to put in a call to Boston IVF to report even heavier bleeding. Back on the chain, I called my mother. She had somehow reached my father in the intervening ninety seconds and he'd told her the news. "Your father is always the first to know," she said.

I apologized and tried to explain, "Dad needs to arrange flights—"

"I'm her mother, Su—" (call-waiting beep).

"I have to take another call—it's the doctor's office calling about my miscarriage." I flipped over. According to the nurse, I am "a pregnancy with a bleed until my next pregnancy test, which is scheduled for Monday."

I didn't feel like a pregnancy with a bleed (I felt like a miscarriage about to embark on a marathon) as I loaded my stuff into the car. I arrived at the hospital just after Meredith had her epidural. I was glad I missed it—I'd sooner take a horse needle than watch them give it to my little sister. Within the hour, Henry's 100-plus-percentile head made its way into the

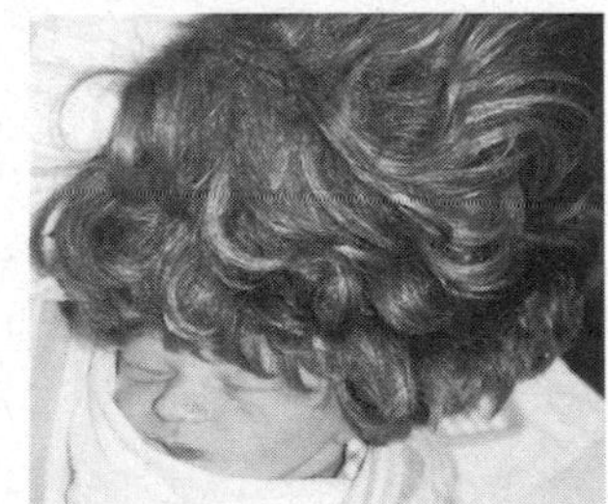

One-hour-old Henry in Grandma Belle's wig

world, followed by a left shoulder, a graceful twist, and the remainder of his twenty inches.

Lorene brought a bottle of champagne over to the hospital after she got off work. We toasted Henry and their new life, as I was surer by the minute that we were losing ours.

I was at the airport before nine the next morning to collect my dad. His extra-cheap airline didn't have any monitors in the arrivals lobby, which fouled up my extra-cheap parking. I couldn't wait for the airline's two employees to agree on the status of my dad's flight. I raced back out, doing a double take as I passed my dad on the way to the curb.

I was sobbing over my windshield by the time he got there. "How much is it, Sue?"

I looked. "Fifteen dollars." He handed me a twenty once we were in the car and said, "Linda told me some of what you're going through, which helped me put everything in perspective. She explained how when you undertake this kind of a thing, the thing you're undertaking, you mentally prepare yourself, you're psychologically prepared for anything." He paused. "I am here this weekend to celebrate being a grandfather."

Wow. I wasn't psychologically prepared for that ending. I adjusted my chauffeur's cap, drove him to the hospital, and dropped him at the doors.

My hCG value went up again Monday, although I was a hundred percent sure my pregnancy was part of the unhealthy fifty percent. On Thursday, nine eternal days after that first test, my pregnancy was declared "abnormal." I was relieved. I was not cut out for another 270 days of a marginal pregnancy. And I was now free to shelve the suppositories. Free to resume my normal activities. I put the garden in. I got back on my bike.

Lorene was grieving. And uncomfortable with the one-week waiting period until we would find out how this abnormal pregnancy would terminate. My belief—that whatever it was I was carrying around wasn't meant for this world—was of no comfort to her. Neither were Meredith and her new baby.

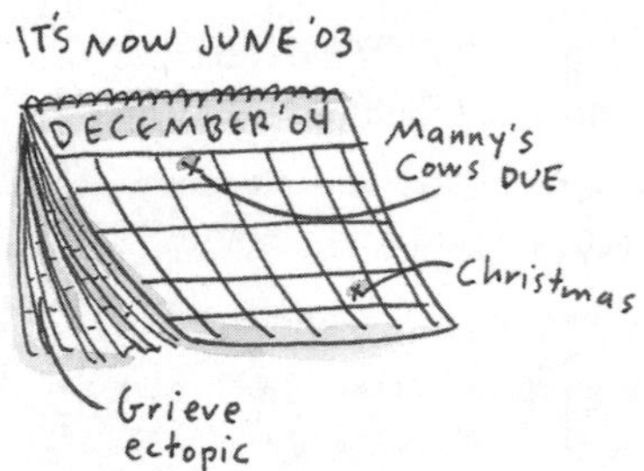

The day before our "resolution" meeting with Dr. Penzias, I went to New York for my rescheduled Cover Girl presentation. The Jell-O brain mold salad I'd prepared set a humorous tone (although I got only two takers), and the tenor of the lunch was generally very upbeat. I made the rounds after lunch, collecting a *What to Expect the First Year* for Meredith and stopping by a college friend's desk. She was now an editor. I gave her my pregnancy update. "That is so weird!" she said. "It was like that with my son."

"Your son?"

"Yep, he was completely borderline for, I don't know, a month, six weeks—seemed like forever."

"Then?"

"Born healthy. Totally healthy kid." I started to rethink everything.

I went into our meeting with Dr. Penzias with a list of questions, my "resolution" resolve wavering. "Do you think we should do more blood work, just in case? I ran into a friend of mine whose thirteen-year-old son was the result of one of these borderline pregnancies . . ."

"I'm afraid yours isn't borderline." Mine had gone further south. "Yours is an ectopic pregnancy." I modified my mental picture.

My options were to have an injection of methotrexate, which had an eighty percent chance of ending the pregnancy; the rest of the time another injection, or a second injection plus surgery, were necessary. Or I could have the surgery straight away. With either option, there would be a three-month recovery/waiting period before we could try again. And neither option would have a negative impact on my chances of "achieving pregnancy" going forward.

"I'm not feeling so lucky," I said to Lorene. "I'll be one of the twenty percent."

"I'd rather you avoid surgery, if you could," Lorene said.

"The shot is the least invasive option," Dr. Penzias interjected from the other side of the desk.

"You could do it now?"

"Francesca can administer the shot right next door at the end of our meeting."

"All right." I was ready to go. Luckily, Lorene remembered our questions.

"Is there anything we can do to improve our chances? Do we know why the embryos fragmented? Did that stain test tell you anything about

the egg or sperm quality? Should we try for better sperm?" Steve was planning to visit over the summer.

"Should I go on the pill?" I added. "And my friend said something about ICSI . . ."

Dr. Penzias smiled. "The stain test didn't really tell us anything. Remember, under the best of circumstances, chances are one in five. Obviously, we are trying to improve your chances, working around obstacles which we've already acknowledged." He leaned forward. "But, there is a silver lining in all of this. An ectopic pregnancy is a pregnancy—evidence Suzy can get pregnant."

We went next door. Francesca gave me a shot in each cheek and apologized, "Your muscles are going to be sore." She also told me to keep out of the sun, which I forgot, then remembered when I felt as if I was going to throw up in the middle of my bike ride the next day.

I spent July and August training for and organizing Ride FAR and working with designers to lay out the brain book. Lorene worked and went for late-night swims while I pored over book proofs. She stopped asking if I would join her. I had become so unromantic. A swim = a drive in the car + getting wet + a wet drive in the car. I just wanted to lie down.

I was lonely. *What about her, do you think she likes swimming alone?* And I felt guilty. This wasn't the life I'd promised Lorene in front of the fireplace a year ago.

I wished I was someone who wanted to swim at night, but as any infertile person will tell you, wishing won't make it so.

In A Parallel Universe

Ride FAR 8 *was a success*. We raised a record $140,000 for HIV/AIDS service organizations, and I was in fine physical form: drug-free since the methotrexate injection three months earlier.

Biking 100 miles a day for 5 days gives you the feeling that you can do anything. *Except the one thing.*

My three-month hiatus gave people plenty of time to reflect on my infertility:

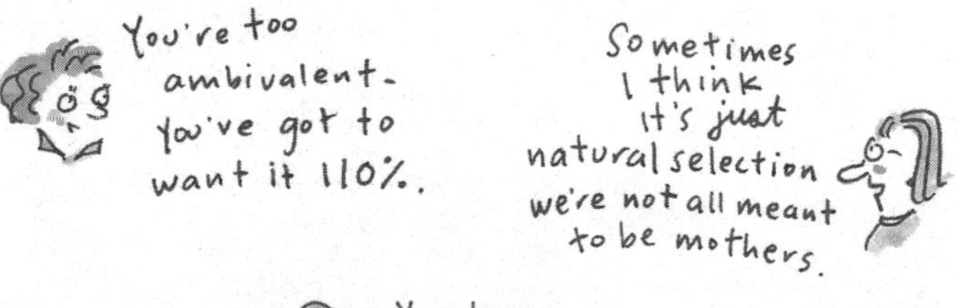

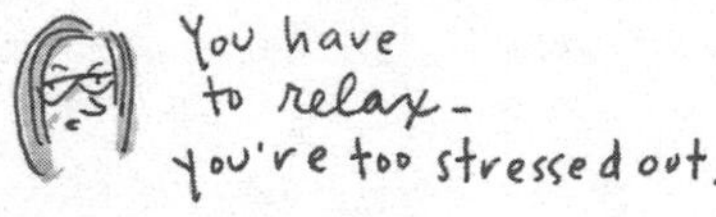

More than one person had asked me why I wasn't adopting. The answer I gave—I wasn't adopting because I wasn't done trying to get pregnant—wasn't entirely honest. (Nothing says you have to give a highly personal question a highly honest answer.) And the answer I gave myself—I was too afraid of the unknowns, the genetics and the physical and mental health histories—wasn't entirely truthful. The truth (which I didn't know back then) was, I was too afraid of the knowns. You begin an adoption, you end up with a child. Some small part of me preferred leaving my outcome to chance.

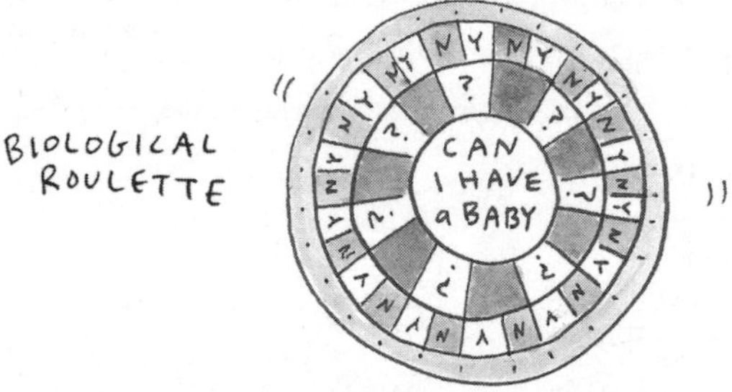

I was ready to get back on the baby project. When I called Boston IVF, I was transferred to the insurance liaison. Now that I was forty-one, my insurance wanted me to "pass a Clomid challenge" before they would authorize more treatment.

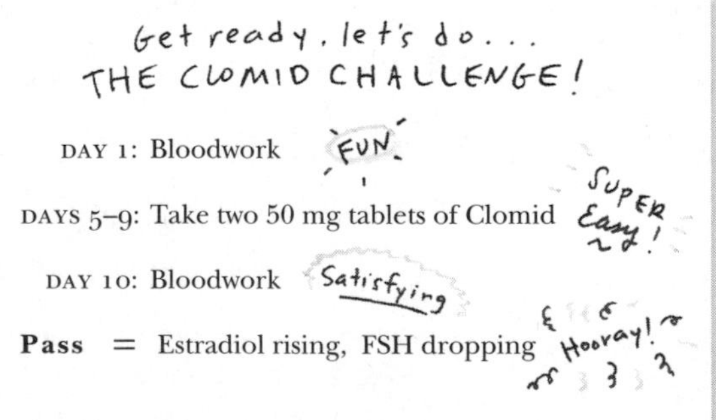

I called a friend on Day 2 to ask her what Clomid was like. "I'm surprised they're putting you on it," she said. "It's for people in their thirties." I wanted to remind her that forty-one wasn't so far out of my thirties, but I explained it was just a test. "I don't remember it being any big deal. It kind of makes you more . . . you," she said. "Higher highs, lower lows. PMS plus."

I felt nothing one way or the other on Clomid. My personal challenge was remembering to take it twice a day. On the third day, the Saturday after our new housecleaners came, I couldn't find my Clomid anywhere. The pharmacy agreed to refill the prescription.

my PERSONAL CHALLENGE: Finding it after I remember to take it.

I was out $54 (small change in the fertility accounting department) but I was still in the game. I passed the challenge. Another small victory, another roadblock circumvented.

In November 2003, we picked up where we'd left off back in May.

The morning before the first ultrasound, a bowl of leftover dog dinner fell off the top of the refrigerator onto Lorene's head. We tried not to take it as a bad omen, but sure enough, the ultrasound was not routine. "Do you have both ovaries?" the tech asked. "Have you had endometriosis?" She shook her head. "Something's going on here."

Techs can never say *what* is going on, but that never stops me from asking. "Something's going on with your left tube," she answered. "Could be a hemorrhage. Could be a cyst. Could be . . . anything, really. I wish I could tell you more." It was enough. Tears ran down the sides of my face and pooled at my hairline as I lay there. Now my good tube was ruined. I'd won the Clomid battle, but I was losing the war.

When we got home, our updated injection instructions were on the machine: stick with the same dosage of Gonal-f, no mention of my tube. When I called back, I was told they were running tests on the blood, but Dr. Penzias wasn't concerned. We were probably looking at some leftover ectopic-pregnancy tissue.

The blood tests didn't allay Dr. Penzias's nonconcern. He ordered another ultrasound and this time he, personally, wanted to do a pelvic exam. The second ultrasound tech identified a "complex cyst" on my left ovary; nothing wrong with my left tube, and she had no problem finding both ovaries. There was a long wait between the ultrasound and Dr. Penzias's pelvic exam, but once I was dressed, he immediately took us into his office.

Cancer Court

"Well, I don't think it's cancer, that's the good news!" *Cancer?!* He spread out the films. "It's a complex cyst; complex in the sense we're seeing solid and fluid. It's reduced over the two days, you can see the fluid is drying up. I'm thinking it could just be an irregular ovulation. I didn't feel anything; you're not exhibiting any other symptoms . . . As long as your levels continue to rise appropriately, I see no reason why we need to scrap this cycle."

"Are we *sure* it's not cancer?" Lorene asked.

"If it's an irregular ovulation, the body will reabsorb everything. We'll keep an eye on it."

I was in my studio when the update nurse called that afternoon. "How'd the meeting go?"

"Okay. Everything's okay as long as the levels are rising—"

"Unfortunately, they're not. Your estradiol is at eighty; it should have been one-twenty."

That was it. End of cycle. Just like that.

Dr. Penzias had a new plan. We would skip trying in December—enjoy the holidays, give the cyst a chance to dry up, and on Day 21 of my next cycle, we would begin a round of Lupron injections, effectively shutting down my ovaries and ceding complete control of my cycle to medicine.

Lorene and I babysat for Henry that night. We went to see the Hugh Grant movie *Love Actually* afterward. No 9:30 shot to race home for. "You were crying," Lorene said as we were leaving the parking lot.

"I know. It was the Christmas pageant. The thought of never having a kid in the Christmas pageant."

She was laughing. "I'm sorry, but did you think you'd have a kid in a church—"

"I'll tell you what I was *also* thinking: For once I wasn't crying about the romance, the thought of never having the big love . . . " I started to cry again. "I feel like I've been this really good sport, having the shots, the tests, smiling instead of wincing . . . What if I turned into the barren-sister-bitch-maniac and kidnapped Henry or sued Meredith for unfit motherhood?"

Lorene rested her head on my arm. "I wish I wasn't so old, I would have the baby for you."

I wish I *wasn't so old.* "It scared me when he said cancer," I said. "It's the first time I really thought about all this stuff I'm putting into my body."

"*I'm* putting into your body. Every time I give you a shot, I think about it."

"One more try."

"Your insurance would pay for at least two more . . . "

"One. If I can, if the cyst goes away, I'll give it one more try."

The next night we were in the car again on the way home from dinner at our friends'. We turned the radio on; scary futuristic music was playing—it was the BBC's *Instant Guide to IVF.* A male narrator was describing the lengths to which some women go to have babies, test-tube babies. More scary music. I looked at Lorene just to make sure I wasn't the only one hearing it, and she flipped it off.

I woke up with an awful headache the next morning. This headache hung on for three days. By the second, I'd forgotten I had a headache and settled into a bad mood, which I attributed to the last and final round of book proofing. And to the town library's *not* getting the roof grant, which I had previously sworn would come as a relief but in reality made me angry about all the pointless work I'd done. And to *Seed* changing the publication date on its next issue, rendering my holiday cartoon useless. And to the Massachusetts State Supreme Court's decision to give same-sex couples the right to marry, which, I know, was cause for celebration, but also took the lid off the very vocal opposition and exposed a lot of the so-called support as disappointingly lukewarm.

con • done *verb.* To forgive an offense

Lorene attributed it to going off hormones cold turkey.

It was December. It was the end of the year in which we had tried to have a baby. While neither of us would admit it out loud, we had stopped believing there would be a baby. I'd like to think we never stopped believing we would be happy without one.

Left to herself, Lorene would have taken time to process the disappointment and grieve the loss of the child we would never have. But she was with me. That kind of time could be my undoing. Instead, she set plans in motion for the construction of our dream studio. Our other life. She brought the carpenter-handyman from a local historic inn over to our barn and the three of us did a walk-through, imagining a porch here, a rope swing and a couple of salvaged doors there.

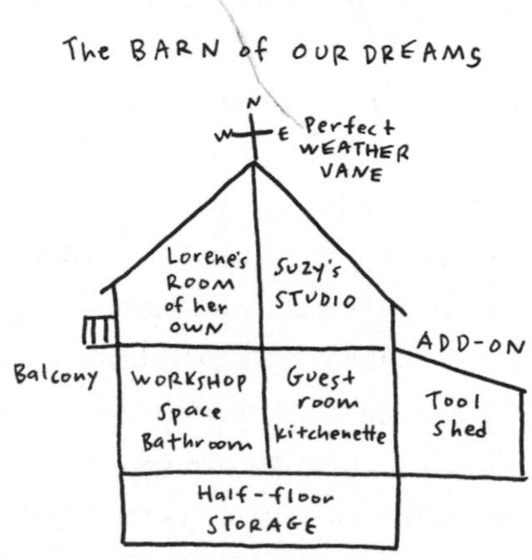

We would live in Bolton another ten to fifteen years. Then, when I was in my fifties and Lorene in her sixties, we'd sell the house and the cars and join the Peace Corps, as a couple, and spend two years working in some far-flung spot. After that, we'd take a small subset of our stuff out of storage and move to the city, where we would go to more movies and lectures and make young friends. I still had some convincing to do.

Oh, the Places We'll Go!

Seychelle Islands
Galapagos
St. Lawrence Seaway
Paris
India
Alaska
Northern Lights
Scandinavia
Copper Canyon

With all the money we never spent on college, we'd travel. Our new friends would look after us in our dotage, the way we looked after our old friends in Bolton. There's no guarantee our child would have looked after us anyway.

Our love would always come first. Our time would be our own. Our late-night dinners, or no dinner at all. Our Sunday mornings. Our weekend getaways. Our spontaneous lunches or middle-of-the-night sky watches. We could be very content being the World's Best Aunts.

HENRY'S 1st christmas

The carpenter-handyman dropped off some drawings. *A rope swing? Poor, pitiful childless people.* We weren't ready to give him a deposit yet.

The Monday after Christmas, I pulled out one last fertility stop.

You go, girl!

I, contrary to my previous public pronouncements that meditation wasn't my cup of tea (or maybe *was*, since I can't stand tea, either), began meditating. It still wasn't/was my cup of tea, but I had been persuaded that the benefits did not discriminate.

I signed up for a one-day Kundalini weight-loss workshop at the local nail salon. At the end of the day, I asked the instructor for a meditation. She didn't have anything specific to fertility or conception, but she was confident the pregnancy and birth meditation, with a couple of tweaks, would work. I secretly meditated for eleven minutes (the suggested minimum) after Lorene and I turned the lights out each night.

NOTE: Yoga and diets—also NOT my cups of tea but I couldn't resist the cartoon potential.

My "SIMPLE HEART MEDITATION"

MINUTE 1: Sit cross-legged and tune in. (lie still)

MINUTE 2: Say, "*Ong namo guru dev namo*" It doesn't matter what it means, just say it. (roughly "I bow to the subtle divine wisdom, I bow to the wisdom within")

MINUTES 3–7: Breathe deeply through nose, eyes closed, focusing on the brow point. Bring awareness to depth of breath.

MINUTES 8–11: Place right palm over heart, place left palm over right hand so hands are crossed over heart. Focus on what you want. Believe it will happen. Feel the joy: *I am pregnant! I am healthy! My baby is healthy!* Or whatever positive affirmation you want to use. (MY ELEVEN MINUTES ARE ALMOST UP!

Journal: January 6, 2004

How did someone who can't draw, has no sense of color or ability to fill a page, get to do a picture book? And the hormones haven't even started . . .

The Lupron injections started up. I got my period nine days later without any of my usual night-before hyperproductivity or day-of slight bloating—my body was on somebody else's autopilot.

Since we tried not to plan our lives around my cycles,* the timing was invariably an issue. This year, however, we had lucked out with the Burlington getaway. I felt a twinge as I packed up the car; I allowed myself, for an instant, to wish I was packing up a baby, instead of arriving at the bed and breakfast empty-armed. My failure wouldn't be lost on the owners, the ones who had sent us off with their best wishes that snowy Sunday a year earlier.

* From Lorene and Suzy's Sanity Preservation Plan, patent pending

When we returned from the long weekend, the real cycle started. That week, I had to travel to New York and give myself the shots for the first time.

I could have continued to give myself the shots when I got home, but I preferred the small ceremony of Lorene's and my 9:30 nightlies.

Dr. Franken did my retrieval this time. He had no memory of our first transfer, which was fine (I still had no memory of his real last name), and there was no need to bring up a sad ending when we could all focus on a happy beginning. He collected a very respectable fifteen eggs in his basket. I slept a full five hours afterward, and I was sorer than I remembered being the first time, but not enough to change our dinner plans.

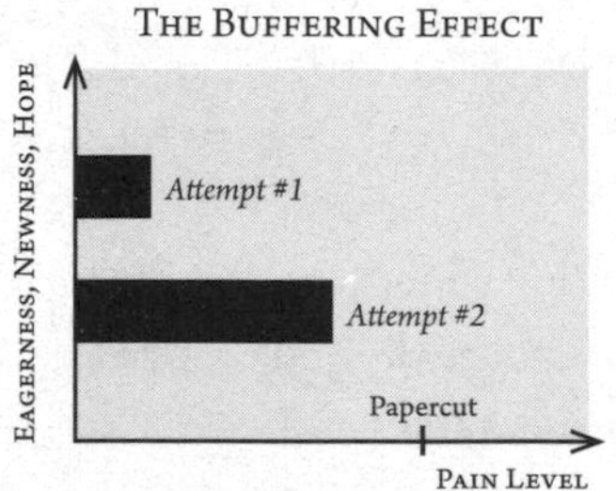

The transfer was three days later, the same day my first bound copy of *I Had Brain Surgery, What's Your Excuse?* was scheduled to land on my doorstep. Fourteen of the fifteen eggs fertilized, but only four developed into embryos.

Lorene didn't sleep the night before. Her anxiety ratcheted way up after *ER*; the episode took place in the neonatal intensive care unit. She was anxious about having a baby, having twins, dropping the baby, forgetting the baby . . . I slept like a baby. Whatever will be, will be . . . over. *Just please not another ectopic pregnancy.*

We met the transfer doctor in the pre-op chamber, a curtained-off cubicle. He was supposedly there to confirm our directives—a transfer of two embryos. Lorene let him know it was our last try. *No pressure.* He closed the curtain and sat down. "At your age"—he glanced at his chart—"forty-one and a half"—*correction, sir, a third*—"you really should consider four or five, given the fragmenting." *Ow!* I felt that in my ovaries.

Lorene and I were not comfortable with the concept of "reduction," a euphemism for aborting if we ended up with more than two. (I know, we hadn't been comfortable with the concept of an IVF eight months earlier, and there we were.)

"The chance of one implantation, let alone two or three—let's be realistic—is small." *Why are we being realistic all of a sudden?*

Lorene now had the doctor talking about his specialty in chromosomally transgendered kids.

What if he's looking for a surrogate?

He returned to the topic at hand. "We have three good-looking seven-cell embryos, a couple of five—"

"Last time I had eights, two eights," I interrupted.

"You are talking about the difference of one cell, a day or less of gestation."

Three sevens. My locker number was 107. Lucky 7.

I looked at Lorene. "You okay with three?"

"I'm okay with three. I'm not okay with triplets, but I'm okay with three."

"Freeze the rest?"

Lorene let me answer. "No, thanks."

We're done.

Outtahere.

This is it for us.

Sayonara and g'bye.

Lorene bent down and kissed me. All the trying would be over when I saw her again.

MEDITATION LOG

~~||||~~ ~~||||~~ ~~||||~~ ~~||||~~
~~||||~~ ~~||||~~ ~~||||~~ ~~||||~~
(440 mins.)

I wasn't the least bit sleepy after the transfer, although I was committed to bed rest, looking forward to it, actually. I read my food magazines, got my meditation out of the way.

At 2:00 p.m., Boston IVF called to report that one of the five-cell embryos had fragmented, making it unsuitable for freezing.

How about our saying we don't want it frozen—
wouldn't that make it unsuitable?!

A few minutes later, I heard a truck slow down and there was a knock at the door. The book!

Your BOOK is <u>not</u> Your BABY

It doesn't gaze back at you.
It is old in three months.
It is subject to very public,
very negative reviews.
It can be purchased for under $30.

Tour de Fetus

A week later—one week down, one week to go until my pregnancy test—I was a nervous wreck. Once again, I was sure I was not pregnant. Once again, Lorene was sure I was. Her certainty was based on my revulsion to olives at dinner. I couldn't convince her that I had simply eaten too much bluefish and would have found anything revolting. The test would tell.

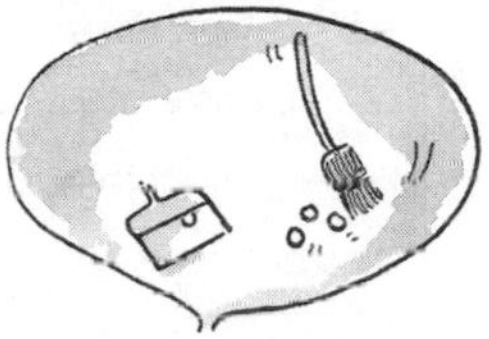

We killed the last four days at my dad's, shopping the wholesale craft show at the Philadelphia Convention Center for Lorene's store, and we were back at Boston IVF, bright and early, for our 7:30 pregnancy test. We had come to know the two women who administered blood tests: the nice one and the one you really wanted to get. I got the nice one. She had me sit up straight and uncross my legs. Then she murmured something about drinking more water as she ran her gloved thumb up and down my veins. She finally finished up about the same time the other nurse dispensed with her third patient. "You'll hear this afternoon," the nice nurse called after us.

I was useless all morning. The review of the brain book in the March issue of Oprah's magazine was just hitting the stands. I checked my Amazon ranking a dozen times over a couple of hours, watching it climb from 65,000 to 25,000 (knowing that anything over 500 really wasn't worth talking about). I went to the bathroom twice to see if I was bleeding. At 10:30, I called Boston IVF to leave my cell-phone number so I could go out to buy a copy of *O* magazine.

My rank was up to 5,000 when I got back. Still no bleeding. No word on the pregnancy test. I called Boston IVF to let them know I was home. In another two hours, I switched them back to my cell phone, as I was getting ready to head in to the public broadcasting station to tape a fundraising spot I had written. Two minutes later, my cell phone rang in the kitchen. "Suzy, we have very good news, a very strong positive! We like to see hCG values between fifty and a hundred—yours was one hundred and eleven!"

I was ecstatic, all of a sudden jittery, quite possibly faint. I held on to the soapstone sink, just in case. The woman had instructions for me, but our cell phones always cut out in the house.

"Six week-ultrasound in March?"

"We count from Day 1 of your cycle." *I was already four weeks pregnant!*

After the call ended, I was still holding on to the sink, looking at the clock, debating whether I had enough time to stop by Lorene's shop to tell her in person, and Meredith called. "I'm pregnant!" I blurted out, and heard how it sounded for the first time.

"Yes! Yes! Yes! All right!"

I interrupted, "Can you bring your *What to Expect* tomorrow? I have to go tell Lorene and get to WGBH."

Lorene knew as soon as I walked in. She came out from behind the counter, arms outstretched. "I *knew* it. I told Ruthie, I had a vision in the shower; we're having a boy! Wait, *very strong positive?*" Lorene said. "Is it twins?" Now she looked nervous.

"She didn't say anything about twins, but you can call her. I have to go. They put me down for an ultrasound the morning I leave for book tour."

"I'll go buy *What to Expect—*"

"Meredith's bringing it."

Lorene's face fell. "You told her first?" She went back to her stool and looked into her computer.

"I'm sorry." I went over behind her. "She called . . . " There was no acceptable apology, no do-over, no changing the fact, not one single satisfactory explanation.

Lorene was subdued at dinner. The nurse had assured her we weren't having twins; she was still upset she hadn't been the first to know.

I lay on my back in our bed. The winter covers felt heavy. I turned them down. Lorene pulled them back up.

I got the news I hardly dared hope for, the news I wanted for how many years, and I feel? Exhausted. "Please," I started. "This whole time I haven't let myself get excited, please, let's be excited now."

"Sorry." She hugged me. "Let's call Steve!"

I felt awful I hadn't thought of it myself. "What time is it there?"

"Is there a bad time to let him know he's going to be a father? I don't think so!" She handed me the phone.

Steve picked up. It was late morning, late for going to work even his time. "You just caught me, what's up?"

"We're pregnant!" He let out a shriek to beat all shrieks. Lorene was laughing again. "We're going to be a family!"

First thing the next morning, I wrote to Mary Ann, our friend the nurse. She wasn't the fourth, but definitely in the first ten to know.

That Monday, six days after I found out I was officially pregnant, my miscarriage fear kicked in. My mother had had several, but she smoked. I was going to be flying to eighteen cities on a book tour—*I see her smoking and I raise her fifty!* I consulted my Boston IVF handout.

THE BIGGEST MYTH IN IVF

Embryos can fall out.
If the uterus was like a balloon, this might make sense. Embryos cannot fall out into a pothole, toilet, etc.

But if the uterus WAS like a balloon you could knot it.

I consulted *What to Expect*.

I consulted Lorene. "You can't cancel your book tour, if that's what you're thinking." I was pretty sure I could; Workman would understand. "I don't want you moping around here. I personally don't think the universe could've come up with a better plan. You just need to make sure to eat and rest—you're going to major cities, not the Amazon."

When I told the publicist, she immediately offered to cancel the tour. "If at any point you're not feeling up to it, you promise to let me know. I'll make sure you have places to rest, late checkout, I'll rent you a room for the day if I have to. Do you want me to tell the tour contacts?"

"Please, no." I had pushed public telling back until after the amniocentesis, whenever that was. The first ultrasound was still a week away. Normal fertile people probably wouldn't even have taken their pregnancy tests yet.

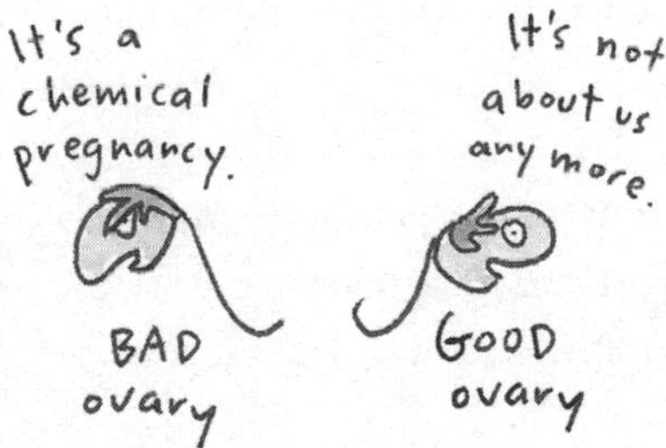

At the first ultrasound, they were looking for a baby, specifically a heartbeat. The technician put the gel on my abdomen. She prepared us as she started searching around: "I may not be able to find it, and that doesn't mean anything, they'll just schedule another ultrasound in a—" We heard it! Over the whoosh, we heard a heartbeat! Next, we saw it! A tiny blinky bulb in the sea of my uterus. "One hundred and twenty-six beats a minute!" We cheered.

I wasn't just hoping so, I wasn't just saying so . . . Lorene squeezed my hand so hard. "Ow! I really *am* going to have a baby!"

"Wow is right!" the technician said.

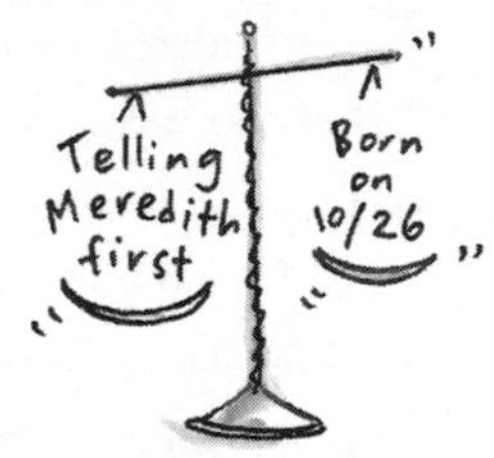

After the ultrasound, we had our last meeting with Dr. Penzias. "Very healthy, seven weeks gestation—due date, looks like October 26th." Lorene's mother's birthday.

"Thank you for everything," I said, which didn't begin to cover it.

"It's all pretty miraculous. The best part of my job." He smiled. "Do you have any questions?"

I asked about flying and miscarriage, miscarriage risks in general, and any miscarriage risks specifically associated with my ectopic pregnancy. The answer was I had nothing to fear. He came out from behind his desk to congratulate us. We were graduating to normal-people ob-gyn care.

I left for Detroit several hours later. My specially purchased one-suitcase-fits-all was twenty-five pounds overweight, so I ended up putting all my shoes, toiletries, and several other items in a separate carry-on.

I promised Lorene I'd let the escorts lift my heavy suitcase, but when Sheila Potts pulled into the handicapped space at the first Barnes & Noble and explained, "I have spinal stenosis, Judy," I knew Lorene would have made an exception.

"It's Suzy," I told Sheila.

Sheila led me to the customer service desk. "I have an author, Suzy Becker, *I Had Brain Cancer, What's Your Excuse?*" Sheila told me how much she'd enjoyed the book while we waited. "How's your husband—wait, hold that thought!" The customer service guy was back. I signed a pile of books and Sheila took me to the café. "You're entitled to a free beverage." I ordered my usual, then remembered the baby, feigned a sip, and tossed it into the next trash can. At least it was free. Luckily, Sheila never missed a free beverage, so I ordered a decaf at the next Barnes & Noble and grabbed a water chaser at the third.

COFFEE LIMIT 1 CUP

When I got to Chicago, I established a routine that worked pretty well throughout the rest of the tour: On arrival, I unpacked and ironed my clothes for the next morning, checked my e-mail, called Lorene, requested my wake-up call, then watched late-night TV until I fell asleep.

I'd do the early show, have breakfast, and then I often had the rest of the morning free so I could exercise nonvigorously (an outdoor walk or a tread in the gym) and do a little work. If you'd asked me at the time, I would've claimed no morning sickness. However, the sight of those book-tour clothes still turns my stomach. And while most food tasted fine, as soon as I finished, I'd make a mental note to never eat whatever it was again, plain bagels excepted.

LET'S NOT DO LUNCH!

THREE stores later . . .

THREE stores later . . .

Most afternoons, I was able to fit in a nap. Then I'd pack up, grab a dinner I could eat on the plane, head to my evening event, and it was on to the next city.

If I hadn't seen the blinking light in my belly, I would've sworn I was carrying this baby in my butt. My boobs, previously sympathetic to the idea of pregnancy, really blossomed, but my stomach wasn't having any of it.

Every few days I considered playing my pregnancy card, but I always thought better of it. Once I said something, there was no taking it back. And it was much easier to not think about miscarrying when no one knew you were pregnant. Besides, assimilating my new public identity as a "survivor" left very little room to contemplate my new secret identity as a pregnant person.

I had never thought of myself as a survivor. True—I didn't die, but all I'd survived was brain surgery, not being stranded on the side of a mountain, left for dead in a park, or extreme poverty or abuse. Meanwhile, I was meeting real survivors by the dozen every day, listening to their stories, unforgettable stories: the postal office employee with brain cancer whose buddies collected a wad of cash ($3,500) and gave it to him on his last day of work, along with their pooled paid leave time (four and a half months). There-but-for-the-grace-of-God-go-I stories; please-e-mail-me-in-two-months-so-I-know-you're-still-alive stories.

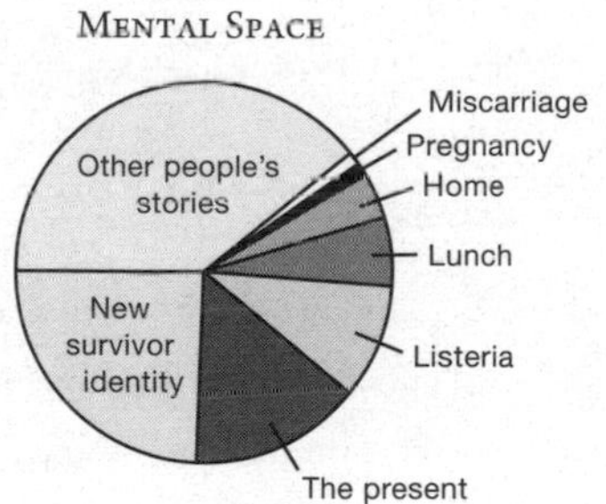

The snow started to fall just after I woke up in Minneapolis. I considered my good shoes, then dashed out of the hotel for a coffee anyway.

Sally, my escort, was waiting in the lobby when I got back. She glanced at my wet hair and offered me a tissue for my runny nose.

"I figured out, we were classmates at Brown," she said. "Don't worry"—just the opposite; for whatever reason, I instantly liked her—"no one ever remembers me."

"Me either," I said. We chatted nonstop on the ride. Between the car chat and the caffeine, I was revved up for my morning show.

Sally's mother called to say she thought I was adorable. "I'm pregnant," I gushed back. Sally hugged me. "It's really too early to tell anyone, but if I were home, Lorene and I would be talking about it all the time."

"Do you want to go back to the hotel and rest?"

"I'm starving!" We ate a big brunch; in between store signings, we visited Louise Erdrich's bookshop. Then it was time to tape a Minnesota Public Radio interview.

The host was Scottish, very nice and very well prepared. My sniffles were an annoyance throughout the segment and I was very close to pressing the mike-silencing "cough" button so I could take a deep, satisfying sniff, when a drip escaped and landed SPLAT on my book. A red pool spread across the passage I was reading. The producer was out of his chair, back with toilet paper in no time. I got the bleed under control, blotted the page, and we did a new take. This time I was afraid to breathe—much less sniff—in. I felt as if I'd completed an aerobic workout by the end of the segment.

Nasal stuffiness, often with accompanying nosebleeds, is a common complaint during pregnancy.

That night I re-created the drama (which had been lost on the radio) for the NPR listeners in the bookstore audience. And then I was winging my way to Seattle, where Lorene would be joining me for the West Coast leg of my tour.

She couldn't wait to see how pregnant I wasn't, but other than that, we didn't have a lot to catch up on. I had called her at least three times a day, and again before I went to bed each night. Even after my page-by-page, she was excited to be on my book tour.

I WAS EXCITED to HAVE SOMEONE...

- to look out on in the audience
- to come back to
- to wake up with
- to remind me to take my prenatal vitamins, drink more water, and not overdo it...

Les, our escort in San Francisco, was Lorene's introduction to touring. He loved the humor in my book, which inspired him to try out some of his own material. "How 'bout gay marriage?" he said, looking for me in the rearview mirror. "Next thing they'll have gay divorce lawyers."

"Why wouldn't regular divorce lawyers work?" I had to ask loudly since the windows were open. His car wasn't air-conditioned.

"You know, she's not a Suzy," he complained to Lorene. "She's more of an Amanda, don't you think?"

He dropped us off at our friends' place in Berkeley. We hadn't seen them since Joshua Tree. Jane was the only person I hadn't been looking forward to telling. She had said more than once that she wanted me to have everything I wanted, but my having a kid would be the end of our friendship as we knew it. "You think you'll be different but there's just no time, you'll see." She and David didn't have kids.

I had told her over the phone before I left on my book tour, figuring we'd return to it in person, but we never had the chance. Jane was beside herself when we walked in. Not about the baby—her cat was missing, and Lorene, Jane, and I spent the afternoon searching and postering the Berkeley hills. As we were leaving, David stopped me on the stairs, "Congratulations, I am so happy for you," he said. "Don't worry, she'll get used to it." Les was honking his horn out front. I hugged Jane on my way out the door and made her promise to keep me updated.

Lorene arranged massages during our downtime in Los Angeles. "When your partner said 'pregnant,' I thought she meant, you know," the massage therapist pantomimed *really* pregnant. She rolled up two extra towels, put one on either side of my middle, then proceeded to reminisce for the hour. "When I was pregnant with my son, I got all kinds of extra body hair. Extra body hair, and my skin cleared up." My old college roommate had told me she craved citrus with her three boys. I was kind of craving wine as she was telling me, but now I filed it with the new information under "Signs You're Having a Boy."

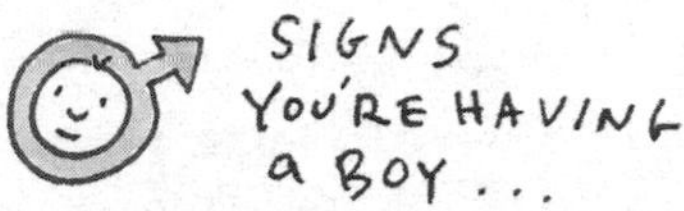

1. You crave citrus.
2. You crave salty foods.
3. You crave meat or cheese.
4. You get extra body hair.
5. Your skin clears up.
✓ 6. You're carrying low.
7. You're carrying out front.
✓ 8. You have little or no morning sickness.
✓ 9. Heartrate ≤ 140

Lorene went home and I soldiered on to the southwest (where I was introduced as "Dr. Becker"), Texas, Colorado, and back to D.C., where Lorene met me again. *The Diane Rehm Show* bumped the book back into the top 500 on Amazon. And then we trained up to Philadelphia.

I had held off telling my dad because I didn't want him worrying about me flying all over; now I was excited to see him. "Pop-pop, guess what?" Lorene said, and she threw open my coat.

He took a step back and clenched his fists. "You did it!" His eyes welled up. "God, you did it." He gathered both of us in his long arms. "Can I interest you two in a late breakfast?"

He pulled into a rib joint that advertised breakfast, but breakfast was over. My dad ordered the pulled pork; the waitress turned to me. My ol' iron stomach had objections to every entree. "Dad, I don't think I can do this," I said. His face fell; I'd never been a quitter. We went down the road and had eggs at a mediocre deli, then my dad took us home. Lorene had a four-hour nap. My dad and I went for a walk.

"I've got to stay on top of my game," he said. He had maintained a regular exercise program for over thirty years, walking or at the gym almost every day since the massive heart attack he had when I was ten. My dad was in great shape, but his heart was a ticking time bomb. "I told Linda I'd like to take my grandkids to Disney World one day." I was sorry that my being an old mother made my dad an old grandfather.

Lorene went back to Massachusetts and I looped through the southeast. I had become inured, didn't blink when my Atlanta escort introduced me as the author of *I Had Breast Cancer, What's Your Problem?* I was in the home stretch. St. Louis, Kansas City, then back to Boston. I was ready to hang up my survivor's mantle and go around the world as a pregnant person.

Lorene met me at the airport, holding up the book escort-style. Vita and Mister were in the back of the car. I —we— were home safe, pending the next ultrasound.

It's A Boy!

Lorene and I were back at the old gynecologist's. It still didn't feel like we belonged. This was a waiting room for women who naturally rested their hands on their burgeoning bellies—for women who *had* burgeoning bellies. Women who relished wearing maternity clothes and went to ultrasounds alone. I sat up straighter and focused on a magazine. "Suzanne?" We were no longer in the land of "Suzy B."

"We'll do an ultrasound first, and then you'll see your doctor," the nurse explained. "Is this your first—" She hesitated. "Yours, right?" she asked Lorene.

RIGHT because it couldn't possibly be UNMATERNAL me!

"Oh, no. Thank you, dear," Lorene said. "My first is twenty-four."

The nurse laughed and handed me a gown. "This is a little like going on a fishing expedition," she said once we were situated. Lorene held my hand as the nurse set the scanner on my belly. "We just need a heartbeat. Now, it doesn't mean anything if we don't find it." *Oh, please, please . . .*

"I hear it!" Lorene said. I couldn't. I couldn't quiet my own heart pounding between my ears.

"There it is!" the nurse found it. "One hundred and twenty beats per minute." I could hear them! "That's what you want. Did you girls want to know what you're having?"

"Isn't it too early to tell?" Lorene asked.

"Look at this." She made an arrow. "You've got a baby boy."

I looked at Lorene; her face had clouded over. "Wait, what about your vision? I thought you knew it was a boy!"

"I know, it's—I guess I was still hoping we'd get a girl." She looked at the nurse. "I already have a son. Daughters are supposed to take care of you . . ."

The nurse laughed. "You can get dressed and head down to the doctor's office."

She left us alone. "Lorene, I was so worried he was gone. I couldn't feel him when he was there, how would I have known if—"

"You wouldn't. But he's there."

"We're having a boy!"

Lorene cradled my face. "Now get dressed, I don't want to make her wait."

"Congratulations! It's very exciting," our doctor said, and promptly yawned. "I'm sorry, I'm giving up caffeine. So, how far along are we?"

"Thirteen weeks," I answered while she scanned my file.

"Now, has either one of you been tested for cystic fibrosis?"

"I haven't." I wasn't sure about Steve.

"It doesn't matter, it doesn't have to be you. How about you?" She looked at Lorene, then went back to the file.

Lorene hesitated. "Me?"

"*Either* one of you—" She checked her own impatience, shifted into explanatory mode. "You need a double positive, so if one of you—"

Lorene interrupted, "My genes aren't really part of this picture." The two of us laughed until it became apparent she wasn't going to join in.

"I'll ask Steve," I said. "But I doubt he's been screened."

"It's the caffeine," she said, and she handed me lab orders. "Have them schedule your amnio on the way out." We got ready to go. "Have you given any thought to your delivery?"

Not a one. We still had a week until we were officially out of the miscarriage woods.

WOODS INFINITUM
CONT'D WOODS P.46
CONT'D WOODS P.20
Amnio Woods
Miscarriage Woods
Fertility Woods
N W E S
CONT'D WOODS P.1
CONT'D WOODS P.24

Lorene had. "As naturally as possible."

"Have you spoken with your neurosurgeon? I will need his okay for you to push." I added it to my to-do list.

From: Suzy
Subject: IT'S A BOY!
Date: April 20, 2004

He's got a good heart (120 bpm), two brain halves, two femurs, two kidneys and two antennae. Just kidding, but he looks, no offense to either of us, like an alien. Have you ever been screened for cystic fibrosis? I'm thinking not. All (it's a lot!) for now, love, xoxo, Suzy

That night, Lorene felt the baby kicking. I would've said gas. *What to Expect* said we were both right; early movements are often mistaken for gas.

"I'm kind of relieved it's a boy," I said.

"I'll love another boy, but I will say, David gave me a run for my money in his teenage years."

"I guess I worry about the two-mom part, you know, not having one of us who can relate to his experience."

"You mean sex? Kids don't talk to their parents about sex."

"I meant all of it."

"Moms raise sons all the time. I raised a son. We have plenty of guy friends. You could've had a daughter you couldn't relate to . . . "

She was right. I'd worry about the amnio instead.

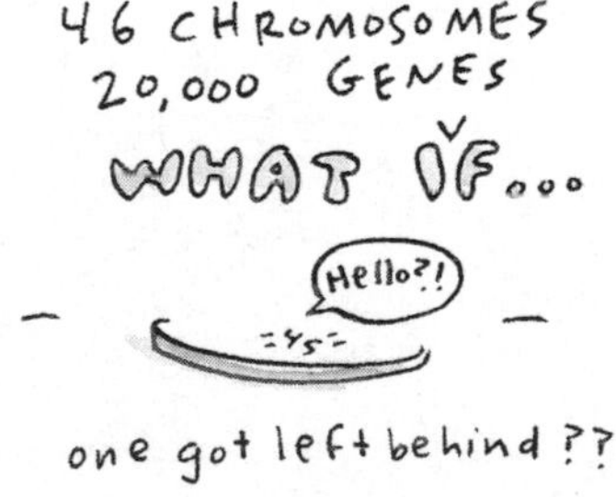

I had a girl. She was beautiful, lying next to Lorene on a white pillow. I went to get my camera and when I came back, their heads were wrapped in turquoise and purple tissue. Just their faces were showing. The baby had little glasses just like Lorene's.

I checked the clock—6:40—and rolled over. Lorene was facing me. "I don't want that woman delivering our baby. Too hurried, too humorless, too—"

"Neither do I." And as long as we were making a switch, I wanted someone who delivered at the hospital where I had my brain surgery, on the very off chance I popped my cork while pushing.

April 16, 2004

To Whom It May Concern,

Ms. Suzy Becker is a patient under my care. From my perspective, it is fine for her to undergo a normal vaginal birth of her child and specifically, I have been asked to comment if it is alright for her to push during delivery. I see no problem with this.

I wish her a smooth delivery and the joys of parenthood.

Warm regards,

John Finn, M.D., Ph. D.

By the end of the day, we were the newest patients of Dr. Bunnell. We had our first appointment two weeks before she was scheduled to perform my amniocentesis, and we both liked her just fine. As she escorted us out of the office, she introduced us to the rest of the obstetricians in the practice since the odds were just as good one of them would be delivering our baby.

Our insurance company sent us our *Healthy Babies* package and we got our first *Safe Beginnings* catalog in the mail. Sometimes it still didn't feel real. We could have been somebody's marketing-list error.

Or maybe I wouldn't let myself think it was real. Not until after the amnio.

It's easy to see why the amnio is a highly over-complained-about procedure:

(a) SIZE of NEEDLE ~3"

(b) *It carries a risk* of miscarriage.*

* Admittedly small, but it's 100% when you're one of the 0.3%

(c) *Your future is riding on the results.*

(d) *It's impossible to get beyond all of the above.*

But if you could, it's really just a glorified shot.

I had attended my sister's, so I knew what to expect. Lorene, of course, came with me to mine. Dr. Bunnell discussed the procedure, and then we waited while the technician found our boy. I looked into Lorene's eyes while Dr. Bunnell prepared to insert the needle. "She's in," Lorene said. I hadn't felt a thing. "She's out." *You're kidding!* It had me thinking, maybe having a baby is an over-complained-about procedure, too . . .

Dr. Bunnell and the technician were laughing at the screen. "Did you want to know the baby's sex?"

"We know—boy."

"Definitely not! She just did three somersaults, spread-eagle."

I forgot I ever wanted a boy, if I ever wanted a boy. I must've wanted a girl all along. I pulled Lorene toward me. "We got a girl!"

"A girl. A girl? Oh, no."

"No? You said you wanted a—"

"Yes, but I raised a boy. I know what to do with a boy. What am I going to do with a girl?" Everybody in the room laughed, and Lorene started laughing, too, wiping the tears out of her eyes.

Boy

~~Dillon~~

Avery

~~Justin~~

Miles

We called Steve before bed, and left a message, "It's a GIRL! Really! We had the amnio today. It went fine. Love you!"

Lorene said, "Oh, thank God."

"What?"

"We would have never agreed on a boy's name."

Three days later, 5:30 on a Friday, Dr. Bunnell called with the results of the genetic blood screen. "Negative for Down's, neural tube defects and Trisomy 18; I wanted to let you know before the weekend. I should have the rest by next Friday or Monday, latest."

On a Scale of Doctors

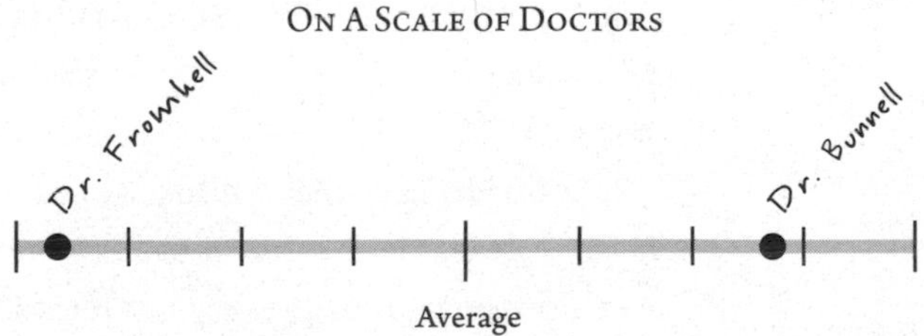

We were at the doctor's. A very cheery nurse started to give us the amnio results and then she stopped abruptly. "I better get the doctor," she said. Our doctor wasn't in. A substitute doctor gave us the results in a hurry, and before they had a chance to sink in, she was interrupted—her daughter (it was Bring Your Daughter to Work Day) needed her. We were shuffled over to another doctor, a man whom I instantly liked. Just as we sat down, he got a phone call from another doctor and the two of them were going on, laughing about a woman who was dying, admitting they shouldn't be. Lorene turned to me and said, "What don't you understand about the results? The amniotic sac is held on by eighteen carpenter ants. One of your ants is facing the wrong way, which is straining the other seventeen, so they will eventually, sooner rather than later, let go. You need to terminate the pregnancy."

I kept myself busy during my waking hours. We had a wedding to go to, our own small second "legal" wedding to plan, and the deadline (my due date) for my first picture book *Manny's Cows* was less than six months away.

Dr. Bunnell called the house at 5:30 the next Friday with the three words I wanted to hear: "Everything is normal." Lorene wasn't home, not reachable by phone—she was helping a friend take prom pictures. I e-mailed Steve and thought about gifting myself a whole pint of Ben & Jerry's, now that I was officially eating for a healthy two, but I settled for chocolate.

> **Chocolate Finding**
>
> Snacking on chocolate can help prevent fetal complications of premature birth in women eating 3+ servings per week.
>
> *Yale Center for Perinatal, Pediatric and Environmental Epidemiology*

Lots of chocolate. Then I filled out a maternity Advent calendar for Lorene. It had been fifteen years since I had made the very first one for my friend, hoping someday there'd be one for me.

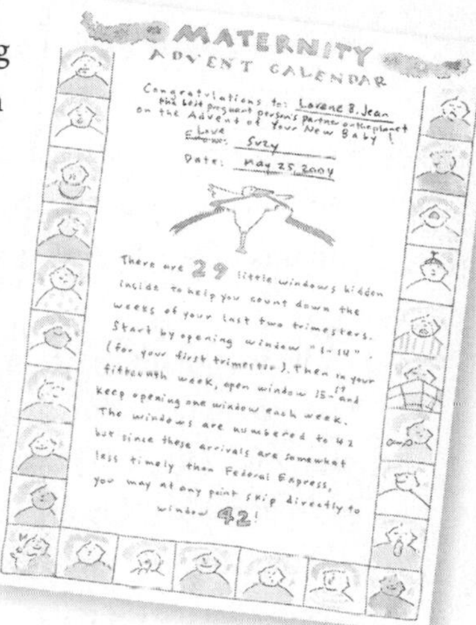

I couldn't wait up for Lorene. My napping time had dried up once I got home from book tour, and I was usually spent by ten. I left the calendar on her pillow. She woke me with a kiss on the forehead, her hair brushing my face. I sat up next to her while she opened the little calendar windows. Then she took me to her closet, rummaged around, and presented me with a bag. A baby dress. I had completely forgotten we'd bought a little dress. Something we'd fallen in love with last spring—possibly for Meredith's baby, possibly for ours. We hung its tiny satin hanger on the closet door of the ~~guest~~ baby's room.

The next week we began telling people we were going to have a baby. Circle the most common response:

(a) Do you know whether it's a boy or a girl?
(b) Congratulations! I'm so happy for both of you.
(c) When's your due date?
(d) What is she going to call you?

The sun went away Memorial Day weekend, and the weather was too iffy to consider a June 1st ceremony underneath the two 150-year-old maples in the backyard. We stood in front of our fireplace. I was barefoot and pregnant in my old wedding dress, standing opposite Lorene in her old wedding dress. There were just six guests, including Henry (in Meredith's arms). We had had our *real* wedding two years earlier; this was our legal wedding.

Jean Eldredge, a retired justice of the peace who'd known Lorene since she was one, had special dispensation to officiate. We repeated the vows we'd exchanged in Vermont, and then it was Jean's turn: "I now pronounce you man—married—a couple!" One of our guests snorted, and we kissed. Then we all sat down to a dinner of poached salmon and Meredith's coconut cake.

The NEW YORK TIMES added SALMON to the Listeria watch List five days later.

The second trimester is supposedly a wonderful time to travel, which was a good thing, because back at Christmas, when we were planning our Other Life, we'd promised my mother a trip to Wimbledon. It was, in all likelihood, my mother's last big trip, given her increasingly limited mobility. Her wheelchair was our ticket to the front of every airport security line. She was seated on an aisle in the row ahead of us; a British midwife was sharing our row.

"She's pregnant," Lorene volunteered.

"She?" The midwife was looking at me. "You're pregnant? Don't look it. Don't look it at all." That was the extent of our conversation, but I felt reassured by her proximity—in the unlikely event I started having contractions, or any other unlikely events.

We put my mother back on a plane after Wimbledon and spent a rainy week on a sheep farm at the tip of a peninsula in southern Scotland. Lorene read *Active Birth* in bed with her coffee. She fell in love with the flavored "crisps"—lamb-and-mint or barbecued-chicken potato chips. I fell in love with British candy. And I advanced to the finals of the peninsula-wide Ping-Pong championships, the only woman entered in the annual summer tournament. Sparing my opponents further humiliation, we never mentioned I was with child.

Later in the week, as we were on a bus barreling down a winding coastal road, I had a thought (over the shrieks of the school-age girls): We could be those foreigners who lose their lives in an obscure crash. Followed by another thought: I don't want to die. But this time it wasn't for the projects and places I wouldn't get to—it was for the baby.

I ♥ MY SWEETIES

CRUNCHIES
DIP DABS
AEROBARS
TREACLE
TOFFEE
MINT CREAMS
SHERBET FOUNTAINS
EAT-MORES
NIBBLES
CHOMPS
WHISPERS

We made our way back to London in our rental car, stopping for an overnight an hour or two from the airport. We'd continued past Stratford-on-Avon—too many tourists carrying too many plastic shopping bags—and found a small inn above a small bar-restaurant in a small village. The two of us watched an old couple take their seats at the table next to us. "Here you go, lovey," he said as he pulled out her chair.

I toasted, "To our next vacation!"

"To true love," Lorene said.

"And happiness," I replied. Our standard.

The couple next to us raised their glasses, said, "Cheers, ole thing," and clinked.

MEET the GRANDPARENTS 2005

We spent the last of our pounds in the airport buying a T-shirt for Lorene's son, a double-decker bus for Henry. "You should get her something," Lorene said. "A souvenir of her trip in your belly."

M'eternity

The last-trimester clock ticked a lot louder than my biological clock ever had. It could've had to do with the fact that it was set to go off like an alarm and not peter out into nothingness. *Nesting* seemed far too cozy a word for my panicked motivation: if it didn't get done *now,* we might be looking at *never.*

THE MOTHER LIST

Have bedroom ceiling fixed
Guest / baby room
New car
Birthing class
Prenatal exercise class
Legal: change will, birth certif.? adoption?
Historical Commission wrap/resign
Manny's Cows
Cartoons through November
Ride FAR 9 prelim.
Hospital Tour
Get Steve's E.T.A.
Have baby

I was intrigued by, but ultimately didn't buy, the notion of "giving birth joyfully" while hypnotized. We chose a natural-birthing class that made a more modest promise to cover all forms of birth experience. I was up for Lorene's natural birth plan as long as the baby and I were healthy, but I didn't want to get too invested. If something happened and we needed a medical intervention, I didn't want to feel like a failure on day one.

> **HypnoBirthing® Class**
> This method of childbirth is as much as a philosophy of birth as it is a technique for achieving a relaxing, comfortable, joyful birth.
> 6 SESSIONS $225

The birth educator at the maternity center affiliated with our hospital was a registered nurse and part-time yoga instructor with ten years of birth-education experience. Having become a better, stronger person as a result of giving birth naturally, she entered the profession to help others prepare for the transformational experience. In her introduction, she intimated that she was on the tail end of another transformational experience, and she and her naturally born child were estranged, but this didn't tarnish the birth experience. It just made me feel a little protective of her.

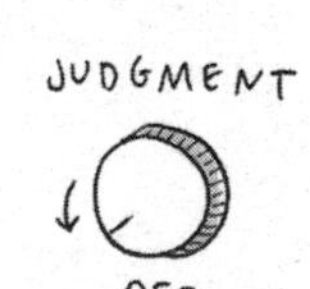

She put a lot of emphasis on the spiritual element of pregnancy and birthing in the first class. "Birthing opens your heart, it has to—your baby's life depends on your heart, your ability to love."

We went over the course outline. In six classes we would learn the stages of labor and birth, and how to prepare for them using relaxation exercises, yoga, mindful breathing, guided imagery, and birth art.

"Birth art?" I had to ask.

She explained we would be drawing our feelings with crayons on paper. Lorene gave a sideways glance to see how I was doing so far. Fine. I had made up my mind to take what I could and leave the rest. Besides, we had already written our names in ink in the birth journal she gave us.

My prenatal exercise class started a few nights later, the same night Lorene worked late. It had been months—ten?—since I'd had any exercise other than walking. I couldn't wait to begin. I ate an early dinner and packed up the suggested water, snack, yoga mat (Lorene's), and a pillow.

The class was held in a meeting room at the local hospital. We set up our mats in a circle. All but two of us were returning students. The returning students (who were a few months further along) readily included us in their camaraderie. They swapped tales of hospital tours and breast-pump rentals, and the two of us newbies listened as though they were the big kids on the bus. I had to remind myself I was the oldest kid on the bus.

After a lengthy series of stretches and warm-up exercises, the instructor asked us to place our pillows on our mats. The real exercise was about to begin: *BUMP PUMP, bring it on!* Then she had us lie down and she led a guided visualization. When we opened our eyes, the class was over.

I kept going to the class and did the so-called exercises religiously in between, but I had to permanently resign myself to getting back in shape after the baby was born. *How long does it take a forty-two-year-old body to get back in shape?*

At our second birthing class, our instructor cautioned us to be careful about our nesting. Rest is very important. At that stage, our bedroom ceiling was being repaired. Lorene and I had moved into the guest/baby room (next on the project list), which was crammed full of our bedroom's belongings, the overflow lining the hallway.

I was reading when Lorene crawled up next to me from the foot of the bed. "That was my cousin on the phone; her daughter had her baby!"

"Everybody healthy?"

"Amazing. She gave birth at home in front of the four kids."

"Wow."

"You know, I think I'm going to take a doula class."

Doula
A woman who provides emotional and informational (not medical) support to a woman during labor

"You should, you'd be great at it." And we both said, "And then we wouldn't need a midwife. Jinx!"

"Would you do it to make money?" We tried not to worry about money, sticking with the belief there always had been and always would be enough—but the brain book wasn't selling as well as anybody had hoped, and Lorene's shop still hadn't fully recovered from 9/11, almost three years earlier.

"I don't think I'd make a lot of money." She opened her book. "I don't know what to do about the shop. I can't work for somebody else and be a stay-at-home mom half the time. I should have—"

"I'M HAVING ONE!" That was birth-education speak for "Contraction, breathe!"

She laughed. "Never mind. I don't like to talk about money before we go to bed." She rolled on her side and put her left hand on my belly. "Remember when you could barely feel the kicks? Oh, those are hiccups."

Lorene enrolled in a weekend doula workshop in the western part of the state. She had twenty-four hours of training over the two and a half days and came back exhilarated, not exhausted. I was glad she was the keeper of the information and all I had to do was follow orders.

You are probably feeling . . . the stretching of muscles and ligaments supporting the enlarging uterus.

I know, it's only *like* a muscle, and there aren't any ligaments, but my brain definitely felt as if it was being stretched a lot of the time, too.

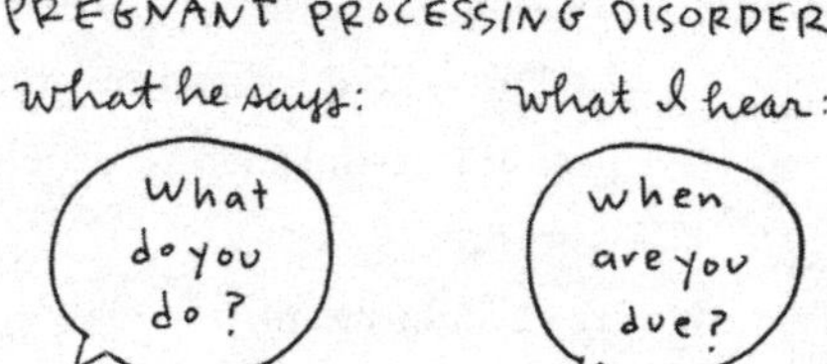

It wasn't the simple preoccupation with being pregnant: I actually felt like a dolt. I had also developed empathy for large-fronted folk who I may have generalized, in my less enlightened past, were sloppier than the rest of us.

On days when I had someplace to go, I was in my second shirt by ten. Otherwise I was sporting a complete meal history, including the lunch I packed for Lorene, by bedtime.

Jane flew in for a visit in late August so she could see me really pregnant. The afternoon we'd spent looking for her cat was life changing. (He came back after sixteen days.) Jane had been volunteering at the Berkeley Animal Rescue every Friday ever since. And whether it was related or not, she'd made up her mind to stay in my life.

I was heading for the door of Terminal B at the same time, on the opposite trajectory, as another pregnant woman. "When are you due?" I asked.

"End of November," she answered, standing there, waiting for me to open the door. The fact that I was also pregnant was clearly lost on her.

I hugged Jane hello, then the first thing I said was, "Do I look pregnant? At all?"

"Definitely." But she hadn't seen the other woman for comparison. I told Lorene about the door incident when I got home. We had asked Dr. Bunnell about my size at our last appointment after I'd noted that the guys working in the cemetery down the road had bigger bellies than I did. Dr. Bunnell had assured us I was "all baby."

"I don't feel comfortable parking in the expectant-mother spots in the supermarket. And just once," I complained to Lorene, "I want someone, not you, to hold a door for me."

Jane suggested that if the opportunity ever re-presented itself, I should put more emphasis on the word *you*, as in, "When are *you* due?"

Lorene shook her head. "It's not your size, it's the way you walk and everything else. You don't look like you want help."

Jane and I had one last child-free weekend. On Saturday we went to Western Mass while Lorene worked. And we spent Sunday with Lorene, picnicking and sunning ourselves on conservation land south of Boston. Then on Monday, Jane hung out with Bruce while Lorene and I went to our birth-education class.

It was our last class, and some of us were still referring to the people who would deliver our babies as "doctors." Our instructor would chide, "health care providers," since others of us had chosen alternative birth settings. Our instructor was still referring to us as moms and dads, and a dad corrected, "moms and partners."

We had achieved our learning objectives; we had done things Lorene claims I could only have done under the influence of pregnancy hormones.

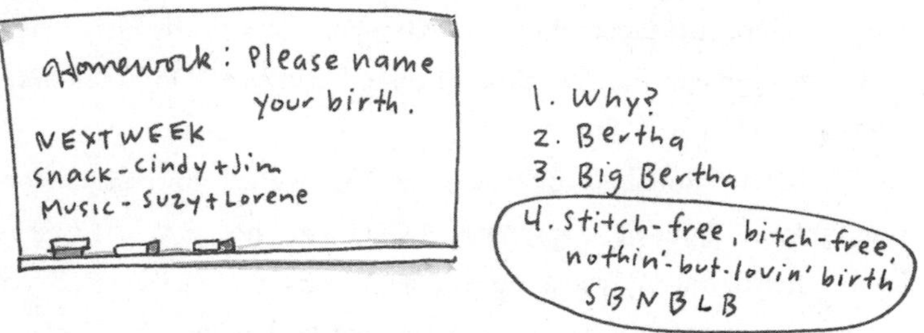

We were asked for one last round of sharing. "I'd like to know what you've come up with for birth rituals."

It was a hot August night and the maternity center's air-conditioning wasn't up to the task. Some of the big-bellied moms were clearly feeling the heat. Lorene finally raised her hand. "Cutting the cord."

"Lovely. You're going to cut the cord." The instructor made a full sentence out of Lorene's answer.

And I'm going to say, "You're on your own, baby!"

As Jane was getting ready to leave, she pointed to a spot in the backyard. "You have to plant a circle of sunflowers for her so she can stand in the middle. My mother did that for me."

"*You* will have to do it. No, I'll do it, and you'll come back when they're six feet tall," I said. She promised she would.

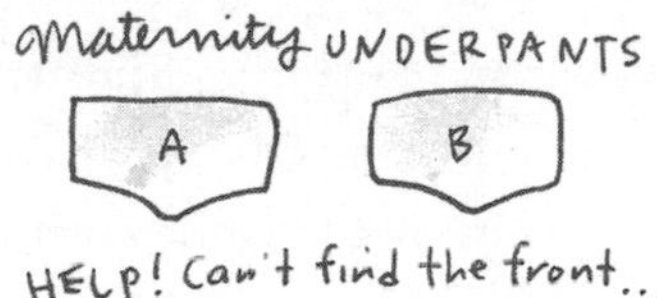

Auntie Lorene and I had a full Sunday of nephew-sitting ahead of us while Meredith and Jonathan went on his company's summer outing. We packed up to go over to their place; it was easier, especially when naps were involved. Dog barking made Henry cry, but he didn't blink when Meredith raised her voice. Meredith said it's all about what they get used to in the womb.

"Our baby won't blink at the sound of a dog barking, and she'll cry at the sound of men," I said to Lorene.

"Now, why would you say that? For starters, our baby has spent every Saturday with your best friend Bruce." *Could be I'm worried about her being raised by two moms.* We weren't in San Francisco or Cambridge, which was fine for us. We could deal with being different. I just wanted everything to be okay for our kid.

It turned out that the company outing was a decoy for our baby shower. *Surprise!* There were twenty-some guests, a game—guess the circumference of my belly—beautiful food, flowers, and a mountain of presents.

HIGHLIGHTS

We were completely worn out from being the center of attention, opening presents, and subjecting other people to present-opening in the sun. Lorene begged me not to work when we got home, but if I inked and painted one page, I was on track to finish *Manny's Cows* by our birthdays, which meant I'd have a full month of maternity leave. A few hours later, I was carrying the finished page down to show Lorene. I missed a step and took the flight of stairs on my back; the finished page never touched the ground. Lorene came running from the other side of the house. "Let me see."

There were welts all down my back. I was crying. "I didn't hurt her, did I?" I whispered into Lorene's neck. *Eight and a half months, oh please, don't let me lose her now.*

We saw one of Dr. Bunnell's colleagues at our appointment that Thursday. We had gone from the every-four-weeks to the every-two-weeks plan. The black-and-blue marks on my back didn't even warrant a note in my file. Our questions may have, though.

Q: Should we be doing perineal massage?

A: Will probably do more irritation than good.

Q: How about breast-feeding classes?
(Most of my yoga classmates were enrolled.)

A: It's like taking a bicycle class without a bicycle.

Q: What do you know about expressing colostrum?

Q/A: Where did we ever hear of such a thing? Nipple stimulation induces labor.

Then Lorene asked the capper. "Do you think my milk will come back?"

"Hmm. Maybe. When was your child born?"

"Twenty-five years ago."

The doctor didn't laugh in front of us. She kindly said, "We usually say five years is a long shot."

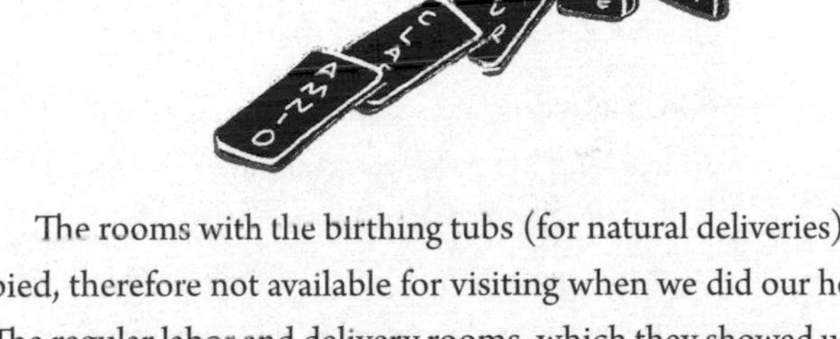

The rooms with the birthing tubs (for natural deliveries) were occupied, therefore not available for visiting when we did our hospital tour. The regular labor and delivery rooms, which they showed us, were hard to distinguish from their postpartum care rooms, which were hard to distinguish from any old hospital room. We got one tip that made the tour worth the price of admission: Request a room with a view for your postpartum stay. — giving up a night at home

Lorene and I had dinner at a deli in town afterward. I was hungry for, possibly craving, gefilte fish. I also ordered matzo ball soup and a pickle, an homage to craving.

"Well, did the tour make it seem more real?" Lorene asked. "Did it scare you?"

"It made the due date more real—it's almost here and we still have a ton to do. I don't think I'm scared. We did the class. You're a doula. Even if my labor is twenty-four hours"—Lorene labored with David for forty-one hours—"it's like Ride FAR. Okay, I don't really know what I'm talking about, maybe it's worse than Ride FAR, but there's an end, and we get a baby." *And even if I was scared, admitting it would only scare us more.* "Are you scared?"

"I'm not scared about the birth. You're going to be wonderful. I'm scared about the next eighteen years. I just didn't know how to help David through school. The public high school was wrong, but I don't know that St. John's was right . . . "

"I feel pretty good about the school part. We'll make sure she gets good teachers, and I'll help out in her classroom."

"Things that weren't hard for me were hard for David, and I didn't get it . . . You think your kids are going to be like you and it's a big surprise, they're not."

"Well, I won't know what to do if she's popular. If it all goes to shit in high school, we can always send her to Steve, remember?" She smiled.

I gave birth to a small baby doll. We were all in the backyard for her naming ceremony, and partway through, her plastic head fell off. I quietly looked around, sure it couldn't have gone very far, but then it was time to hold her up and I had to make an announcement. Everyone helped us look, but no one could find it. Someone suggested it wasn't a big deal, any baby head would do, they're very easy to replace, and I felt relieved because I realized it was true.

Lorene and I went back to Vermont for our birthday weekend. We wrote up our birth plan and we met with Julie, the officiant at our Vermont wedding, to put together some kind of a naming or welcoming ceremony in early November, the Sunday before Steve would head back to Melbourne.

Robin met us for a birthday dinner in Shelburne Falls. She had made us bracelets.

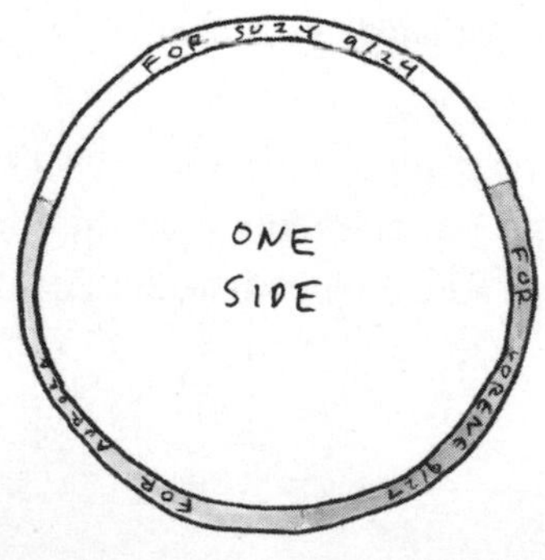

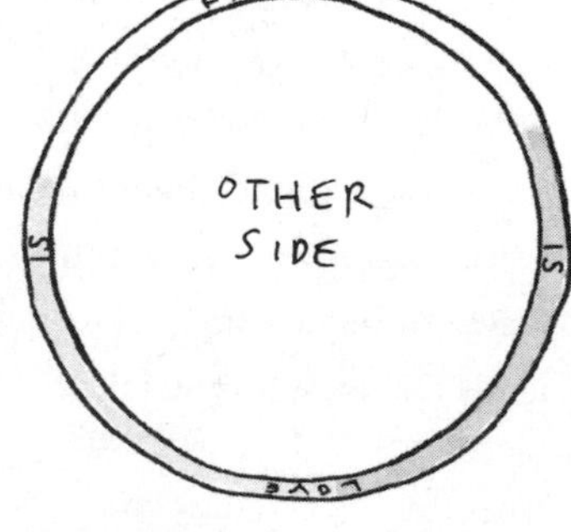

"I'm not going to make these for anybody else, not with the three kinds of metal." There were tears in her eyes when we thanked her. "I'm sorry, I feel stupid. We're celebrating your birthdays."

"That's fine, I'm trying to forget mine," said Lorene. Her friends, plenty of whom were grandmothers, didn't hesitate to tell her she was nuts for having a baby at fifty-three.

"I'm worried I'm going to feel left out. The only one without children. You and Meredith will bond even more, the kids will play together . . . " She wiped at her eyes. "I really miss Meredith. We used to talk every night when we were making dinner, but at least I felt like I still had you two."

It made me sad she didn't have someone of her own. "You'll still have us. It's not like Meredith and Jonathan; we work for ourselves. We may not be able to get out this way as much, but you can always come see us. And Mommy still calls her guest room your room," I joked.

"See? Stop it. The two of you will have your kids and I'll be taking care of Mother."

Our last morning in Vermont, I was squatting in front of the refrigerator naked, surveying the remains of our weekend provisions, and I sneezed. "These pelvic floor exercises aren't working," I yelled to Lorene. I had switched my weekly exercise outing from prenatal exercise to prenatal yoga at the end of the session, but I had kept up the daily "workout" at home.

"You should be doing Kegel exercises all the time—do them when you're standing in line at the supermarket." Lorene had the camera.

"Oh, no. No, no, no."

"What? Your baby is going to want to see pictures of your belly."

I never saw pictures of my mother's belly. "My baby is *not* going to want to see pictures of her mother naked."

"She won't mind seeing you naked until she knows you are naked." I cooperated for two pictures, and then we took the Sunday paper back to bed. After we finished the paper, we caught up on *What to Expect,* reading and napping most of the day.

"Look, it says people have sex to relax." She peered at me over the tops of her glasses.

"I relax to relax."

"That's good, because I think we're both coming down with something."

I couldn't get sick; I had to hand the artwork for *Manny's Cows* over to the editor when she was in Boston in exactly two Saturdays.

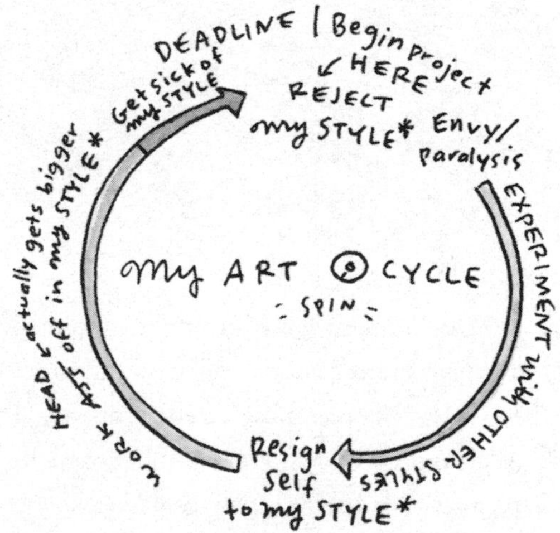

BIRTH PLAN

Ideally, I would like to:

Go into labor spontaneously, rather than be induced. If induction is necessary, I would like to try natural methods, using pitocin as a last resort.

Stay at home as long as possible, allowing 45 to 75 minutes for travel depending on traffic.

Have a room with a birthing tub. Remain active during labor with no internal monitoring and the minimum of external monitoring. Eat and drink if I feel like it to maintain strength. I may want to deliver from a squatting position or be given a choice of positions.

Avoid all forms of pain medication.

Try to reduce the likelihood of an episiotomy (having my perineum stretched/massaged with warm compresses and oil and other means).

Avoid forceps and suction device assisted delivery, but prefer suction to forceps if necessary.

Be as alert as possible with Lorene present, if a Cesarean section is necessary.

Have my baby placed on my chest immediately after birth, facilitating breastfeeding/postponing non-medical procedures for as long as possible and when possible, I would like procedures (exams, bath) performed in the room.

Room in with Lorene and the baby. We would like a room with a view.

Ideally, Lorene would like to:

Be as involved as possible—catch the baby? cut the cord?

We went over our birth plan with Dr. Bunnell at the thirty-six-week appointment. "So, we don't want an anesthesiologist in the room," I explained. "Much easier than refusing their offers," our birth instructor had advised us. Lorene and I had an understanding: If I asked for pain medication three times, she would find the anesthesiologist.

Dr. Bunnell was on board with the plan. She reminded us to bring another copy, in case she wasn't with us in the delivery room. Lorene asked if she could "pull" our baby out when the time came and Dr. Bunnell looked at her quizzically. "When I had my son, my doctor asked me if I wanted to, and I reached down under his arms and pulled him out. It was amazing."

FAMILY PLAN:
we have one every 25 years.

1979

2004

Dr. Bunnell smiled. "Let's see how we're doing, but I don't see any reason why not."

There was another delicate matter. I brought it up. "There's kind of a complication with the birth certificate. We want both of our names on it and Steve is okay with that—"

"Steve's the dad," Dr. Bunnell confirmed.

"Yep, and he's going to be around for the birth, but we've been told not to mention he's the dad at the hospital—there's some sort of professional obligation among the staff to report biological fathers because of deadbeat dads and everything."

"The birth certificate will go through with both your names?"

"We hope so." It wasn't clear. The hospital would send the certificate over to the Department of Health, and according to our lawyer, they were eager to get it. The state hadn't come up with a policy since they'd legalized gay marriage in the spring. The Department of Public Health would then forward the certificate to legal, and after that it was anyone's guess. They could sit on it. They could send it straight through. They could attempt to identify a father and make us go through with an adoption. Lorene, Steve, and I found that eventuality depressing; Steve and I would have to sign over our rights so Lorene and I could coadopt her.

I never got a cold after Vermont, but Lorene ended up with pneumonia. I brought her lunch in bed. "What have *you* been eating?" she asked, brushing the crumbs off my shirt.

"Oh, prenatal deluxe grahams." I liked to insert "prenatal" in front of any food I ate. "Listen, I'm going to the appointment alone today—you're staying home—and I'm skipping yoga tonight." We were now on the once-a-week plan, and this appointment was with the one colleague we had yet to meet. I knew Lorene was really sick when she didn't object.

Dr. Middleton may have been last, and shortest, but not least. She measured my belly twice. "You are forty-two years old." I nodded. "You do not look forty-two." It wasn't a compliment. "Your baby is small; three to four weeks small. You look so young, no one has been paying attention to your advanced maternal age." Dr. Middleton was about to make up for it.

She had me hooked up to a fetal monitor. Three minutes in, the little needle went flying off the tape. The baby had the hiccups. When the hiccups had not gone away by minute seven, Dr. Middleton took me off the machine. "Your baby's heart rate is one sixty!" I overheard her low-talking "infant tachycardia" in the hall. Sign it's a girl!

"I want you to go to the emergency room." *Do not pass Go, do not collect $200.*

"The emergency room?"

"Your baby may do better outside your womb. Once it's out, we can take care of it . . ."

"Can I call home?" She handed me the phone. After I finished explaining, Lorene asked me to put the doctor on.

I handed the phone to Dr. Middleton. "Her name is Lorene and she is home with pneumonia."

"How far away are you?" Dr. Middleton asked. "Well, even if they induce her right away, you should be here in time for the delivery."

"I don't think she should drive," I said. Not in rush hour, not with a fever, not when I was the one who did our Boston driving, but Dr. Middleton had hung up the phone.

I drove myself to the hospital a few blocks away and handed over my file. "Dr. Middleton was concerned about my baby."

"How are *you* doing?"

I changed into a gown and they put me back on a monitor. No more hiccups. SCORE ONE for the SCARE CURE!

A nurse came in after fifteen minutes to read the tape. "How does it look?" I asked.

"Perfect, but Dr. Middleton is very smart. If she's concerned, it's not without good reason. I'll check again in fifteen minutes."

Another nurse popped her head in. "The doctor wants an ultrasound, SGA. Someone will come take her down when they're ready."

I watched TV. And the clock. 6:15. 6:30. *Lorene should be here soon.* The monitor checker apologized, "They're always backed up down there."

"Could I get a snack?"

"I'm sorry, your doctor doesn't want you—" Just then I saw Dr. Bunnell, *my* doctor, coming down the hall.

"C'mon, let's get you out of here." She started unhooking me from the monitor. "I don't know exactly what triggered this—the baby may be a little small, but by the time you get an ultrasound and some resident reads it in the middle of the night . . . "

"What's SGA?"

"Somebody said something about SGA?"

She shook her head, "I would be shocked if—" Lorene walked in. Dr. Bunnell put her arm around her. "No emergency, you can take her home. I'll have the office schedule an ultrasound Monday—Monday's a holiday—Tuesday."

SGA

Small for gestational age: constitutional or pathological

IGR

Internal growth retardation: physical growth slow, mental growth appropriate, risk for hypoxia, hypoglycemia

"I had to get our neighbor to drive me—" Lorene started to cry. "God, I am just so happy to see you," she hugged me. "*And* you," she patted my belly, "and you," she squeezed Dr. Bunnell's arm.

I drove us home. "You could still make it to yoga," Lorene said. "The relaxation would be good for you."

The irony of shoehorning yoga into the end of this day was irresistible. I don't know that I would have had the self-discipline not to tell my toxic hospital tale in the sacred space, but I wasn't given any opening. That night we were invited to share exactly one word. The word that best described the little being inside us; the word that would describe her forever since we, as mothers, had already come to know her spirit intimately.

Small. I tried to think of another word in between *luminous, joyful, curious, wise, teacher,* and the ten others that were taken in the turns before mine.

"Compact." I'd said it. I couldn't take it back. I couldn't qualify or explain it. I could only hope that my baby was busy or sleeping and hadn't heard it.

The Home Stretch

I met my editor and her husband in Concord and turned in the art for *Manny's Cows.* She took the pieces out one by one and admired them on her picnic blanket. Turns out, she began apologetically, she would be seeing Manny into, but not through, production. Her husband had accepted a job in Chicago and they would be moving. She had plans to enroll in divinity school, and the two of them had begun the paperwork—they were going to adopt a baby.

How could I begrudge her? It was a glorious fall day, and at the conclusion of our picnic, I was officially on maternity leave!

I stopped in and poked around my favorite antique shop on the way to the car. A framed embroidery sampler caught my eye. *Schmaltz city.*

Lorene and I switched sides of the bed; I gave up the wall side so I wouldn't wake her when I got up to go to the bathroom. And the Middleton affair had given me insomnia, so I also had to try not to wake her after I got back.

WEE HOUR VISUALIZATION

Making my UTERUS more HOSPITABLE

Our baby aced the Tuesday ultrasound. She scored eight out of eight on her "biophysical profile," whatever that was. Her weight (five pounds, eleven ounces) was in the bottom tenth percentile, but we were *on* the charts. We had a very healthy baby with a low birth weight. Dr. Bunnell told us that one of her daughters weighed under six pounds at birth, and by age five, she was in the 95th percentile.

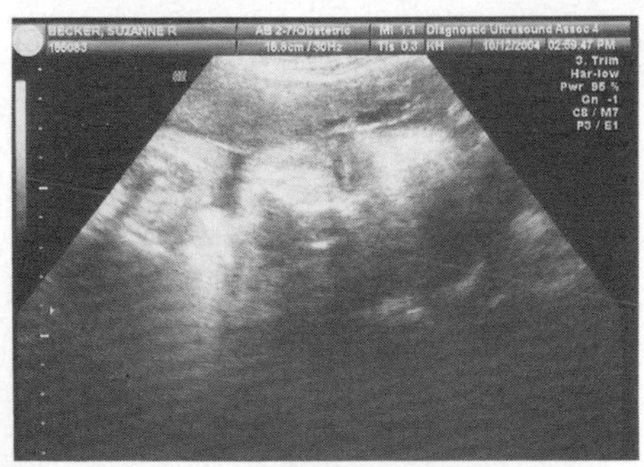

Now SHE HAS REAL not ALIEN EYES

My uterus, however, was not off the hook. I would need another ultrasound in two weeks to make sure the baby was maintaining or gaining weight; if not, they would induce labor.

"Two weeks? That's when you're due anyway. Do we want to wait two weeks to see whether she's gaining weight?" Lorene asked as we were leaving the building.

"Dr. Bunnell seemed fine with it."

"You should've been having these ultrasounds all along; we were worried about your size—we would've had a baseline."

Thank God, Jehovah, or whomever I hadn't had all the ultrasounds! I would've spent the entire pregnancy living in fear from one to the next. "Do you want to call the birth instructor and see what she knows about low birth weights?"

We hadn't spoken with her since the summer. She was happy to hear from us.

"Is that what they're telling you?" she moaned. "They've got no research, no data to back up this claim that babies do better outside the uterus."

Data or no, they certainly had more experience dealing with low-birth-weight babies than my uterus, but we decided to believe in the instructor. Worrying couldn't possibly be good for the baby or the uterus.

We spent the last few nights before Steve arrived putting the finishing touches on the nursery, which was also his room. It bore no resemblance to the Pottery Barn baby sanctuary I'd envisioned—gleaming white furniture and me, on a sliding rocker in the corner where the guest bed now stood. But "when-since," as Lorene would say-ask, is anything in our lives gleaming white? There were a half dozen Hefty bags full of hand-me-downs waiting to be put into the bureau, changing table, closet, and attic. The night-light spun orangey-yellow stars on the ceiling from where it sat on the bureau. This was our soon-to-be real baby's real room.

The Nursery

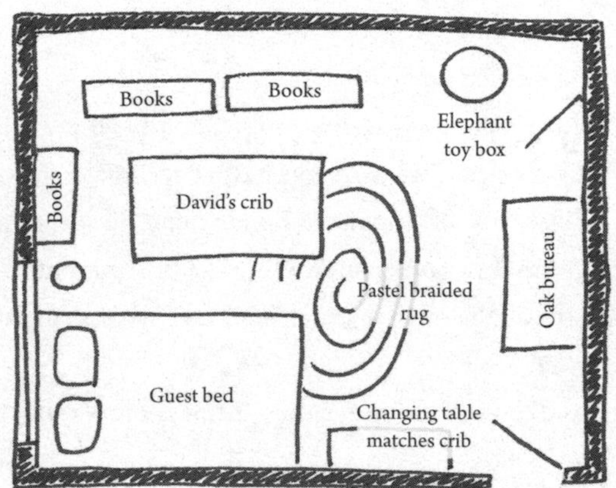

Our last night alone, we packed our bags for the hospital and stowed them by the kitchen door. Mister sniffed the bags. "That's right, your life is about to change!" Lorene told him. He sat looking expectantly at the biscuit door. She gave both dogs biscuits and we went to bed.

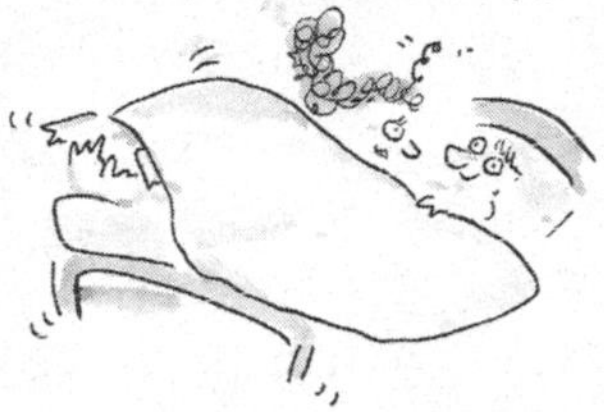

GOING STRONG in WEEK 38

"Just so you know, if I wasn't so tired, I'd consider, you know—it's not that I don't have desires. You look so beautiful, and I'm never going to get this body again," Lorene said. She kissed me and turned out her light.

I didn't have desires. *And* I loved her so much.

We had dinner out on our way to the airport. Our last romantic dinner for the foreseeable future. We ended up staying until closing time. Our waiter had kids and, like most strangers, he didn't hesitate to warn us about the mess we were getting ourselves into. "It changes everything—there's an understatement. Are you ready?"

"I think we are," Lorene said, relatively confidently. *After we change the wills, winterize the garden, freeze a bunch of dinners . . .*

"Love the new car," Steve said first thing, after the hugs were done. I laughed, recalling the one we'd picked him up in the last time.

"We've got two new, well, one used-new—" Lorene had opened my coat.

"WOW!" Steve stood, just looking. "Can I?" He placed his hand on top of my belly and let it rest there. *I wonder whose hands she'll get.*

It was a clear night, just like the one we'd had three years ago. Less of a chill in the air. We took our same seats. Three years seemed like such a long time; then again, they were still working on Logan. Steve gripped the handle above the window, a crutch (not a comment on my driving) for someone who was used to gripping a steering wheel when he sat on that side. "I always knew," he said, pivoting on the handle to face me. "I knew you'd get pregnant."

I didn't. I never knew. I wished. I hoped that planning and praying and saying it out loud would make my wish come true, but it was so easy to imagine Steve saying the exact opposite just then.

"She pulled it off," Lorene chimed in from the backseat.

"You both did," Steve said. "So, am I sleeping in the nursery?"

"Nursery–guest room. We kept the bed."

"I was thinking I should probably stay somewhere else after the birth."

"She won't be sleeping in your room—"

"No, well, I was thinking more about you two needing time to sort things out . . . "

"It'll be we three," I said. "That's all the time you'll have with her for a while, unless, you know, you decide to move next door. Well, next door's not for sale, but . . . "

Steve's old routines came right back to him. The late-night wanders. Late-morning breakfasts, afternoon dog walks, and late-afternoon snacks. We made dinners together, and as long as there wasn't a Red Sox game, we hung out in the kitchen until ten or so, then left Steve to his late nights. There seemed to be a newfound comfort, a familiarity (Lorene and I admitted we missed the shrieks; even the dogs didn't seem to faze him). Or maybe edges had been softened now that we had all passed the pregnancy achievement test.

The Red Sox were in the American League championships. Lorene and I were "closers" (her term)—we could give a fat rat's ass about the rest of the season, but we never missed a play-off game. I was sure we could get Steve hooked, from a gambling angle, but he couldn't be bothered to try to understand baseball. He was channeling all of his betting energy into our presidential election, which he couldn't get anybody else to bother with. On play-off nights he would shut us in the living room to work on his novel and talk on the phone at the kitchen table.

The morning after Game 5, there were two tea mugs in the sink. "Looks like Steve had a late night," I said to Lorene. She was stacking up his note piles and setting them to the side of the kitchen table.

When I came down for lunch, he was just getting out the juicer to start his citrus routine. "Sleep okay?" I asked.

"I got a few hours." He cleared his throat, part of the citrus process. "Yeah, look, I'm feeling a bit . . . I don't know." He sat down and eyed his piles. "I don't think this is going to surprise you, I'm feeling a bit stir-crazy. You're used to being out here in the middle of nowhere, you like it . . . " He stalled out. I waited, trying to decide whether I was surprised or in denial or whether they were mutually exclusive. "Look, I'm totally dependent on you guys for transport, for everything. I just don't think it's good for any of us."

"I don't really feel your dependence," I said, which would explain why I hadn't gone out of my way to make sure he was having a good time.

"I talked to Bruce last night and he invited me to come stay at his place for a few days or a week or whatever."

Here we fuckin-go-again.

"Oh. So what's your plan?"

"I'll catch the tram in West Concord." *Train, you idiot.*

"I could have the baby any day . . ."

"I want to be there," he said.

Now that he'd said it, I pictured him *there*. "Did you mean there, like *in* the room?" Reality has always been the problem with my imagination.

"Nah, well, up to you, really. You've got Lorene and Meredith." As he was saying that, I remembered the whole thing about the birth certificate. He went on, "I think I did, but I can't imagine I'd be of much use. I don't know what I'd do."

"You can be right outside, first one in . . ."

"Yeah, that sounds about right." *Phew.*

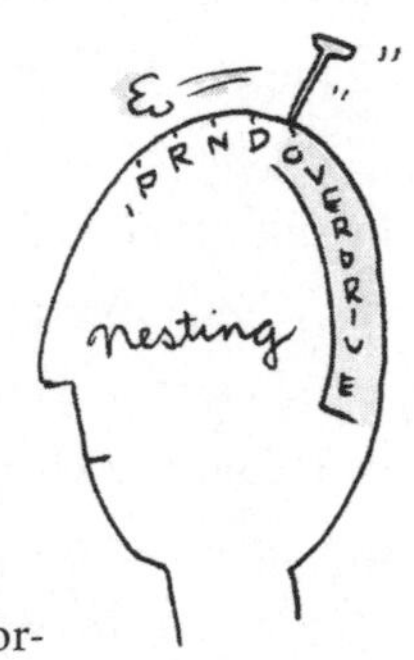

After Steve left, I became the pregnant person I'd read about but never thought I'd have time to be. I was sure I'd have a preemie, like myself (six weeks) and Meredith (four weeks) and her son, Henry (two weeks). I thoroughly cleaned the refrigerator and stocked the freezer—cooking, apportioning, packaging, and updating the list of premade dinners tacked to its side. Every day felt like a bonus.

FIVE OUT OF 100 WOMEN GIVE BIRTH ON THEIR DUE DATE

American Congress of Obstetricians and Gynecologists

My dad called. "Suetta, what do you think about my flying up this weekend to be there for Tuesday, the big day, right?"

I hated to squash his enthusiasm, but I didn't need an extra set of expectations hanging around. I pictured my cervix clamping up. "Would you stay at Meredith's? Dad, I'm not dilated at all. There's no chance of my having this baby over the weekend. How 'bout I call you after my Monday appointment?"

> We believe everyone, the developing baby included, has a right to an education. With your help, your child can start life as a successful graduate of our prenatal stimulation program.
>
> Dr. VandeCarr, *Prenatal University, Hayward, CA*

He decided to stay put. Steve came home for the weekend and he left us with a big pot of his potato-leek soup when he went back to Bruce's on Sunday night.

All the women in my yoga class were reading to their unborn babies, which the instructor said was wonderful. I confessed I wasn't. She encouraged me, at a minimum, to talk to my baby. Out loud. *What if kids have a quota, a number of words after which they stop listening to their parents?*

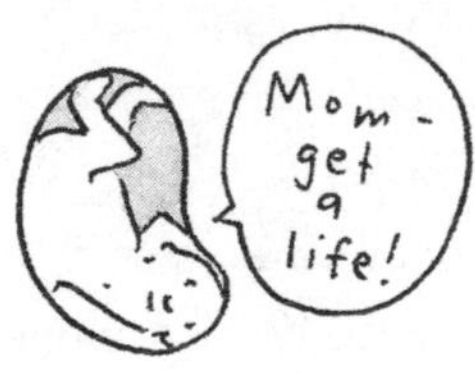

I don't think I could've felt any more bonded. We'd gone from being co-inhabitants to silent partners, especially since that last ultrasound. I know I said something if she had the hiccups or kicked me (her womb outreach), but I felt completely self-conscious when I decided to give her a pep talk the morning of the next ultrasound.

I stood in our bedroom and looked down at my belly, clasping it like a ball, and I said out loud (to distinguish it from some self-conscious silent praying I'd been doing earlier) in age-appropriate words (steering clear of threats like "Pitocin" or "cesarean"), "Be big. Be healthy." Then I added, "Eight out of eight," just in case she got my competitive genes.

It worked, or she did it anyway.

She gave us the eight again, and she'd gained thirteen ounces, moving us up to the 12th percentile.

However, I was still zero centimeters dilated the day before my due date. We asked Dr. Bunnell for some dilation advice. "Have you tried castor oil? It tastes really awful—that's how it works. It nauseates you." We hadn't tried anything yet, but we were ready to.

Lorene asked, "What about nipple—"

"Nipple twiddling. That's a serious time commitment. Twenty minutes an hour." *Never mind.* Dr. Bunnell wanted to see us again in a few days; she could not, in good professional conscience, let the pregnancy go more than another week at my advanced maternal age.

We bought the castor oil on the way home. Maybe it'd work the way the baby-extractor did for our contractor's wife in the delivery room. One glimpse of them rolling it in, and the baby came flying out. I saved my castor oil receipt, just in case.

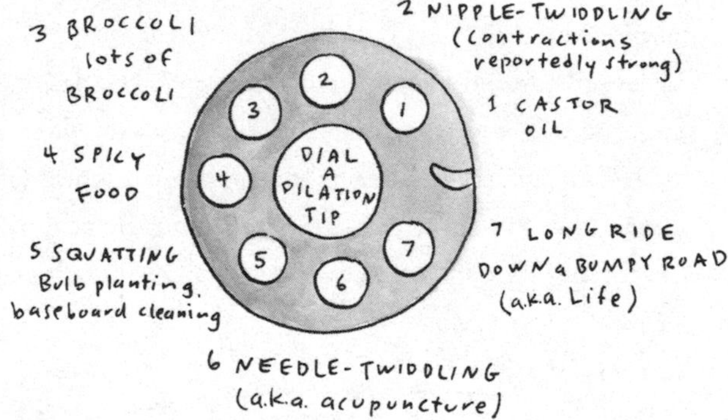

We signed up for some needle twiddling. Our friend's acupuncturist (the one who had righted one of the twins when she went breach a few days before delivery) could see us right after our next appointment with Dr. Bunnell. And we gave Indian food a try.

On the way home from our spicy dinner, I called my dad with the non-news. "Do you think I should get an absentee ballot?" he asked.

"Dad, I don't know. I have no idea—I think you'll be home in time for the election." Although as I said it, it sounded implausible. It was hard to believe I'd have a baby by then. Or ever.

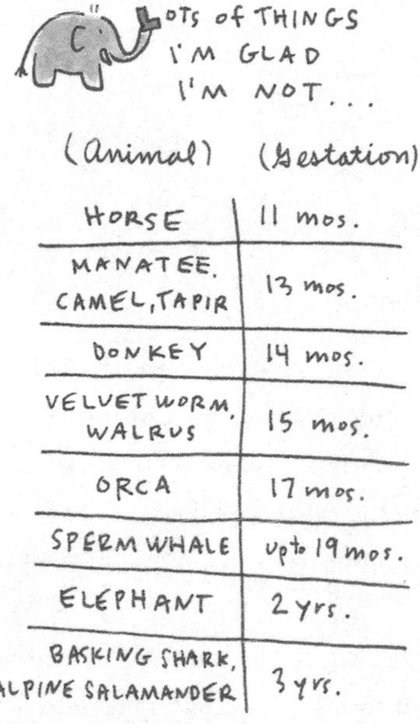

(Animal)	(Gestation)
HORSE	11 mos.
MANATEE, CAMEL, TAPIR	13 mos.
DONKEY	14 mos.
VELVET WORM, WALRUS	15 mos.
ORCA	17 mos.
SPERM WHALE	up to 19 mos.
ELEPHANT	2 yrs.
BASKING SHARK, ALPINE SALAMANDER	3 yrs.

The night before our next appointment, we went to watch the fourth game of the World Series on the big screen at the old movie theater in the next town. The Sox had won the first three. Johnny Damon led off with a home run and we were all out of our seats. A twelve-year-old boy jumped up and ran across the stage, swishing a broom back and forth, as we all chanted, "SWEEP! SWEEP! SWEEP!"

"Maybe we should call her Jonetta or Ortizia," I said to Lorene.

The Sox won the game. The curse was reversed. 2004 would make history, a very auspicious year!

I was three centimeters dilated the next morning. I didn't feel any different. "We could get things started, make sure you keep progressing," Dr. Bunnell offered. It was her euphemism for Pitocin. We shook our heads no. "Then I want you back in here tomorrow, and I'm making an appointment for Saturday at the hospital—we're closed here—in case we need to induce you."

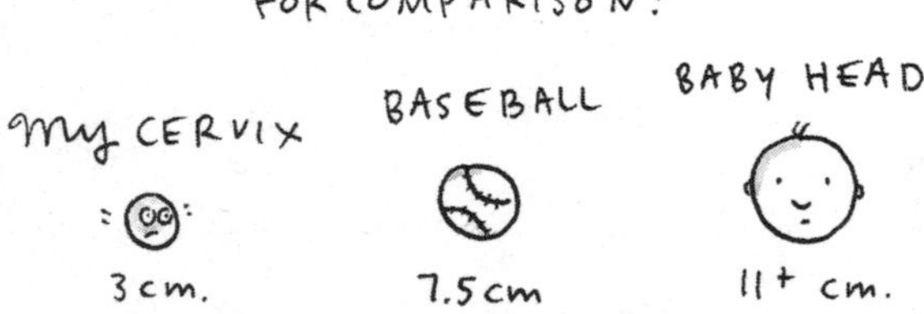

The acupuncturist's office was in a fourth-floor walk-up in Jamaica Plain. It was a beautiful, Indian summer morning, the first sun we'd seen after a run of gray, November-type days. I was silent-talking to my core, not singling out my cervix, as we hiked up the stairs: "Let go, let gravity," I repeated over and over; it ran counter to all the years of "suck it in, suck it in."

The acupuncturist walked us through her kitchen to her office. I filled out a series of forms, and after she reviewed them, she asked us if we had any questions. Lorene specified our outcome: We were looking for labor within twenty-four hours. The acupuncturist smiled a noncommittal smile. I considered asking whether you had to believe in it for it to work, but I didn't want to diminish her belief in me. She led us to a table in the middle of the room where she actually did the work and had me remove all but my undergarments and lie belly-down. Lorene and I admired the retro reflexology posters that hung on all four walls.

The needles were whisker thin. I didn't feel a thing when she put them in, took them out, or during the forty minutes in between. There was one in each hand—the muscle between my thumb and my forefinger—and the rest were in my calves, ankles, feet, lower back, and right shoulder.

The only thing that stung slightly was the alcohol in the Sharpie when she marked the spots on my lower back that Lorene was supposed to massage during labor.

The acupuncturist did some acupressure massage on my shoulders and lower back; we gave her our $90 and a hug and were gone. "Rest!" she called after us on our way down the stairs.

I stopped and called back up, "Is it okay to take the dogs for a walk?"

"As long as it's restful," she said, and we heard her door shut.

"That means no stop at Babies'R'Us," I told Lorene. We had planned to eat macrobiotic on our way home, but we couldn't resist our old fertility haunt, Matt Murphy's Pub.

At 5:30, after we got back from our dog walk, we went upstairs to read and rest. "Feeling anything?" Lorene asked.

"I'd tell you," I snapped. About fifteen minutes later, I felt something that felt something like a menstrual cramp, but on second thought, maybe I just *wanted* to feel it. And how would I know if *it,* being the first thing I felt, was anything or not? A while later, I felt a second. The third one lasted a minute, so I mentioned it to Lorene.

"Shit. I left the chart and my watch in the car." She got up to get it.

"Don't. It's probably nothing."

By 6:45, we were sure they were contractions and we were arguing over the length of time in between, since we still weren't writing anything down.

"Let's go downstairs and have some dinner, while you still have an appetite," Lorene suggested. I added some spinach to Steve's soup, and we each had a bowl. Then I put the finishing touches on the spaghetti sauce I'd left on the stove and packaged it up.

A Couple REGRETS:
Lorene's - we smelled like spaghetti sauce.
Mine - I added spinach to the soup. (came out my nose later.)

I called Meredith to let her know we'd be heading in to the hospital, stopping to pick her up in the middle of the night. Then I left a message for Bruce and Steve.

Lorene rolled the big exercise ball into the kitchen. "Want to bounce?"

"It's really starting."

Hold on, TIME OUT!

NO! KEEP GOING! A woman of Advanced Maternal Age must ~~never~~ think STOP.

The phone rang; my freshman-year roommate was calling. I explained about the contractions, and she was happy to distract me, reporting out on her first marathon. About ten minutes into the conversation, I was unable to finish a sentence.

Lorene snatched the phone and told her, "I think we'll be going to the hospital now." She called Dr. Bunnell's office, called Meredith to scratch the pickup, snapped one last picture of me looking annoyed and pregnant, threw a towel onto her passenger seat (in case my water broke), and we were off.

A Room with a View

We arrived at the admissions desk at 10:30. I gladly accepted a wheelchair even though other contracting walk-ins continued on their own two feet through the doors and into the birthing center. When I was examined, my cervix hadn't budged. Three centimeters and holding. I was evicted from my wheelchair and ordered to walk the hospital halls in my johnny for the next two hours.

These are for you Nurse- they're still warm. I popped them in after my water broke.

(19 cm. dilated)

Meredith, Lorene, and I circled the floor, making stops for contractions. I took to resting my forehead on the cool wall, swaying left to right, saying "EEEEEEEEEEE" at a decibel that caused my head to reverberate, drowning out a good portion of the pain. It was only a matter of time before I had one opposite the elevator doors.

Modesty CLIPBOARD

I was initially afraid of being sent home, stalling my labor, Pitocin, or a C-section. After an hour, I didn't care. I just wanted to be able to sit down, lie down, or take a bath.

I was finally admitted at 1:00 a.m., a paltry four centimeters dilated.

Our nurse, Linda, picked the nicest room for us—not one with a tub. Both tub rooms were free—I was guaranteed a tub when the time came, but the tubless rooms were much more spacious. I didn't mean to harp on the tub, but it was a key part of my visualizations.

Linda explained how the tub-room transfer would take place: "We can only fill it once, so we don't want to fill it too early or it'll lose heat. Figure it takes fifteen or twenty minutes to fill. You just let me know when you're ready."

I decided to hold out for transition, use it to get me through the worst part. There was an LED board displaying the word EPIDURAL continuously in my brain, but the word never crossed my lips.

Transition
The short phase of labor marked by the most powerful contractions just before the pushing stage

A couple hours later, I still had two or four or four thousand centimeters to go until the magic ten when I could push three times, just like Meredith, and get this baby O-U-T. I called for the tub. In twenty minutes, we shuffled down to the new room. I looked for the cedar closet, and then I spied the "tub"—a freakin' kiddie pool, on the floor, on the far side of the bed. The water was ankle deep and the hose wasn't feeling any deadline pressure. I lowered myself to a full sit in order to take advantage of the water level, and BLAMMO! Major contraction. I couldn't stand. I couldn't sway. I couldn't get out of the freakin' tub. The sides folded in on me when I tried to hoist myself up. Lorene considered coming in, then she tried a lower-back massage. "DON'T TOUCH ME!" I screamed, and forgot to smell her hair.

I'd had it. I couldn't take any more. Nurse Linda refused to measure me, she insisted she'd *know*—when my voice got really guttural. Nurse Linda called the doctor in; it was Dr. Bunnell's colleague who was eight months pregnant herself. She informed me I was ten centimeters dilated *and* I was beating the second-time mother next door. "Are you ready to push?"

Oh yes, I am. I am ready to push. Three times. Or ten. NOT one and a half hours.*

I had tried everything—sitting, squatting, hanging—and nothing seemed to be working. I gave up and resorted to lying on my back again. "There's her head!" Nurse Linda wheeled a mirror over. "Do you want to see?"

I *knew* if I could see her little eyes, I'd—"Ew, oh gross, no!" I closed my eyes. There was nothing resembling an eye in that mess. *Oh, God, I hope those words weren't her welcome to the world.*

"Not yet, not yet, not yet, NOW! PUSHPUSHPUSH!" I squeezed my eyes tighter shut; I squeezed everything as hard as I could. "There she is!"

* 1.5 hours is well within range, although I had blocked out the upper end of the range

I opened my eyes. Lorene was lifting her up by her underarms. She laid her on my chest.

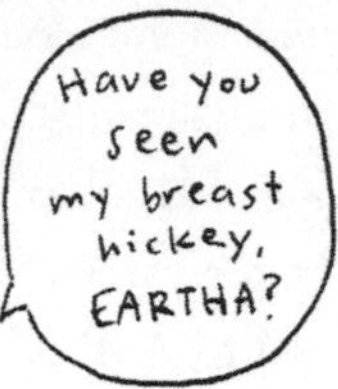

I looked down in disbelief. Not your garden-variety Miracle of Life awe. She had latched on to my left breast (not the nipple, a situation that Nurse Linda rectified once we all emerged from our postdelivery stupor) and was peacefully suckling. *Wait, this isn't my baby. My baby, my baby, the one I've been carrying around for forty weeks and three days, is a dark-haired, red-faced screamer. Lorene must've pulled this one out of the drawer under the table while I had my eyes shut.* I was looking at a beautiful baby—fair-fuzz hair, pink skin.

"Does she have a name?"

"Aurora," we said. "Aurora Jean Becker."

After all the years of dithering, wishing, waiting, it is unremarkable as far as birth stories go. I labored a very average eleven hours. There were no complications, for me or the baby, not counting the tub. I left out my water breaking (somewhere in the shower sequence), and there will be no mention of my "mucus plug." Everybody else seems to leave out the afterbirth.

While Aurora was tranquilly nursing, I had to push out the placenta. (The third stage of labor and the second-most-underpublicized part of pregnancy, after the ten-not-nine-month gestation period.) It left the room before anybody had time to request a doggie bag.

We said good-bye to Nurse Linda—her shift was ending—and there was a sudden rush to get us over to the postpartum unit. Some other delusional laboring mother must have wanted our tub.

Lorene held Aurora while I showered in our new room. I double-padded the supersize mesh underpants in my self-care kit and pulled my sweatpants up and over. "It makes a nice package," I said to Lorene, grabbing my crotch as I entered the room, and I heard my dad's laugh. He had Aurora nestled in his arms, sitting in a chair at the end of the bed.

"She's quite a package," he said, gazing down at her. "I couldn't wait. I booked my flight for this morning and I talked to Jonathan after I landed. He had me take a cab to the hospital."

Steve and Bruce were the next to arrive. Bruce stood back while Steve held his daughter. Then

WHAT WE PACKED

- snacks
- boombox and CDs
- small lamp and outlet-splitter
- favorite pictures of nephew and step-son
- lip balm
- ✓ oil for peritoneum
- playing cards
- book
- birthplan

✓ = WHAT WE USED

NOTE: Birth education classes don't really prepare you for your first birth. Nothing can. It doesn't matter, the baby will be born. Aim for a false sense of preparedness, pack whatever brings you peace of mind. I am not ashamed of the playing cards.

Bruce cradled Aurora while Steve peered at her out of the same fog of disbelief. Just about three years ago, he had handed someone some jars and now, here she was!

My mother appeared with a boxful of pastries. My sister Robin and Aurora's "brother" David rounded out the day's visitors. Visiting hours ended at 8:00, and everyone was gone well before then. At a few minutes before nine, Lorene looked up and said, "Look who is . . . "

Dr. Finn, my neurosurgeon, stood in the doorway, his surgical mask hanging under his chin. "I hear congratulations are in order," he said. Lorene handed Aurora over; Dr. Finn smiled at her and then snatched off her cap to inspect her skull. "Perfect, just perfect. C-section?"

"No! 100% natural, awake baby delivery!" He'd bought Aurora a bunny from the hospital gift shop. I had to catch myself or I'd start believing he was worth it, the brain surgery, I mean.

Lorene stretched out on the fold-out chair-bed by my bed. "It wasn't even twenty-four hours ago," she said. I looked at the clock. When I turned back, she handed me a small box. "For the amazing mother of our beautiful daughter."

"You're the most amazing partner," I said. (Not so original, but consider the sleep deprivation and perineal trauma.)

She laughed. "Meredith and I both said you could've had her in the middle of the woods, saying, 'EEEEEEE' against some tree."

I shook my head and pulled Lorene to me with my baby-free arm. "I was way too scared to do this alone."

That first night, we were awakened for various checks and tests. Lorene would go with Aurora and report back. With each "pass" (and intervening nap), my confidence mounted.

"Her ears are perfect!" Lorene announced as she rolled Aurora into the room. Her ears *weren't* perfect; it was plain to see that one looked like a rooster's comb, but a nurse had assured us that ears are made of cartilage and it would continue to fill in over the next few weeks.

"She was an amazing partner, too," I said. Aurora's heartbeat was rock-steady every time they'd strapped a fetal monitor onto me, and she nursed two of her first three hours on the planet. She was still in the size dregs, but we were never interested in becoming percentile parents.

I went downstairs to get us good coffee on Saturday morning and got back to the room just as they were broadcasting the nursing-bathing-class reminder. Lorene grabbed Aurora, I held on to the coffees, and we headed back to the elevator beyond the front desk. "Hold up—let's see some ID, please!" I looked behind the desk to see who had said it.

"We're just going to the nursing-bathing class downstairs," I said, pushing the "down" button.

"Oh, no. No, no, no, no, no. Your baby is not allowed off this floor until you go home. You shouldn't even be in the hall without one of those carts. And whichever one of you is going, you're going to need some ID to get back on the floor."

I'd made it back onto the floor with nothing but sugar packets in my pockets when I'd gone to get coffee. Lorene preempted any further conversation. "Let's take her back to the room. I'll stay, you get your ID and go to class." So I breast-fed and bathed a pretend baby *like taking a bicycling class without a bicycle* while Lorene watched our real baby. And when I got back to the room, I breast-fed our real baby while an underemployed lactation consultant bestowed the La Leche League seal of approval upon us (me, my breasts, and my baby).

The Red Sox parade shut out all visitors until late afternoon. We watched the parade coverage and napped. I wrote. We had our meals brought up from downstairs; we could've been staying in a hotel staffed by nurses.

Dr. Middleton handled our discharge the next morning in a surprisingly perfunctory manner. I felt compelled to draw it out. I asked her a question about baby care; she gave me the not-my-department "ask your pediatrician" answer and was gone.

HOROSCOPE

LIBRA ♎
Everything is turning out in your favor. Don't stop while the momentum is building. Give it your best shot and follow through with your plans.

us

SCORPIO ♏
Look over your personal papers and get things in order. You will have to act fast. Preparation now will save you time later.

Aurora

For all its empowerment, natural delivery did not exempt me from the wheelchair exit. I was pushed down with Aurora in my lap, and the three of us waited curbside for our car to come around. The car seat was checked for proper installation, then we buckled our baby in and pulled out from under the overhang into the late-morning sun.

Lorene was driving, checking the rearview mirror every tenth of a mile; I craned my whole self around the passenger seat to look at Aurora every third check.

REARVIEW to REARFACING
come in rear-facing...

We got off the highway one exit early to pick up some milk and the Sunday *Times,* passing by Hudson Art & Framing on the way. "It's a girl!" was painted in big pink letters across the windows.

"That's Ma's shop, peanut," I narrated.

DO-OVER!
Going home Outfit for Baby

Lorene pulled into a parking space to have a closer look. "Geez, it's Halloween—I completely forgot!" I had, too. It could've been spring *or* fall. We could've been gone two days or two months.

Lorene pulled back out onto Route 62. A half mile later, a pickup crossed the double yellow line right in front of us, careening up onto the sidewalk—beside us for an instant, then gone. We kept going. "Aren't you going to stop?" I asked.

"There's somebody right behind us." I craned again; the pickup was safely stopped on the sidewalk. We were silent until the next turn. "I'm sorry," Lorene apologized. "I'm too shaky to help. I just want to get us home."

"If we had left the shop one second earlier..." In those instants I always conjure up all the near misses we never even know about.

We took our baby and our paper and went straight to our bed.

There were still three hours until the dogs were returned and the dinner guests arrived (with dinner).

We lay there propped up on pillows, with Aurora sleeping between us, and I knew I should have been thinking how our lives had changed forever, so I tried. But it was way too soon to know how, and I preferred feeling as if she'd always been there.

The phone rang. Aurora didn't stir. Our friend Susan Anker couldn't hold out any longer. She was coming over. She piled onto the bed and held Aurora as though she was her own, until Aurora started crying.

"Hungry, I think," I said. "Hide your eyes." I didn't care about my ninnies; I didn't want her to see the hurts-like-a-bastard face I made when Aurora latched.

As I was pulling up my supersize mesh underpants a week later, the absurdity of the idea that we were about to host a naming-day ceremony for sixty people entered my mind, and then exited, embarrassed, as quickly as it had entered. Steve had come home two nights earlier to help us get ready and spend his last few days with his daughter. We collected anointing water from our town's Little Pond to add to the water Steve brought from Australia's Port Phillip Bay. Prepared food. Bought wine. Cleaned the house.

Everyone was gathered between the two old maples in the backyard. The sun was warm, directly overhead. Our baby's first no-hat day. She was in a christening dress that had been in Lorene's family since the nineteenth century. The three of us stood with Julie, the officiant, facing our guests. Steve, my mother, my sisters, David, and Bruce up front. Then Susan Anker and our friends who had wanted this baby with us—the village that would help us raise our child—gathered behind. The thought, the sun, looking into all the faces, made me well up.

We had just about finished cleaning up and cramming the last of the food into the refrigerator when it was time to take it back out for dinner. Steve's farewell dinner: leftovers. Aurora was sleeping in the sling. Lorene set the table. Steve put on dinner music.

"Will you take some more photos of me with Aurora tomorrow? Nana June will eat them up."

"We'll get you up early; there's a nice light in our room," Lorene offered. Steve didn't say anything. Lorene nudged him. "You okay?"

"Me? Oh, fine. Look." He pushed his plate away from the edge of the table. "You two've got the major adjustment ahead. But leaving is hard. It was hard the last time, and she has a very strong pull, that little one."

"Oh, c'mon, stay!" Lorene said.

"Please, Daddy?" I whined.

"Stop it! If it weren't for my parents . . . and Mark . . . Never mind." He got up to change the music. "Last-night dance party!"

It was only nine, but Lorene and I were ready for bed. Steve would be up all night packing, pacing, having his tea and cereal. We had a few dances and said good night. Then I went back downstairs to give Steve the compass necklace. "We'll get it when we're in Melbourne. Or you can bring it back before—" He lowered his head, and I centered the compass on his chest. He had been listening to 10,000 Maniacs.

"Natalie Merchant's always reminded me of you," he said.

"She had a baby," I said. Just like that, without envy, without wondering whether I ever would. "G'night, honey," I said, and we hugged good night again.

The next morning we got Steve up with us. By 11:30, we had accomplished breakfast, the photo shoot, and the trip to the post office to ship his suitcase overflow back to Australia. Everything was looking good for a one o'clock departure to Boston, making stops at Old Navy for Mark's presents, and a three o'clock appointment at the hospital, where Aurora's birth certificate was waiting to be signed and sent back over to City Hall.

Steve was headed into the bathroom for a quick shower about the time we were sitting down for lunch. "Listen, don't worry about me, I'll make myself something, or I can always grab a bite at the airport." He was still in the shower when we rolled Aurora out in her all-terrain stroller for a walk with the dogs.

A little before one, we got back and Steve was popping a couple of pieces of bread into the toaster. He got himself a plate and had a sit-down lunch. I went upstairs to change Aurora.

When I came back, Steve was reshelving his lunch makings in the fridge. He slinked by in his slippers to finish up his packing. "Don't say it. Don't say it; I'm hopeless. I'm just not very good at these transitions, you know."

It was three on the dot when we arrived at the hospital and valet-parked the car. "Want me to stay down here?" Steve offered.

"Maybe they'll add a third line to our certificate," Lorene said, and pulled him onto the elevator. It was a nonappointment, nonevent; someone asked our baby's name and handed us the birth certificate. We signed and handed it back. Our mute tagalong smiled.

"You okay with it?" I asked Steve when we were a few blocks from the hospital.

"No question. You two *are* the parents. I would have absolutely no idea what to do with her at this stage."

"You'd figure it out," I said. "Feels kind of dumb, inadequate, saying it again, but . . . thank you."

"Thank *you*. You've changed my life. Made it much better, really."

We killed some time at the airport, lingering this side of customs. Then Steve walked backward through the passageway, waving until we could no longer see him.

It was just getting dark, a hush coming over the day. Aurora was hiccupping in the back seat. *The one who used to be hiccupping inside.* "It feels good to be home, just the three of us," Lorene said as we walked up the garden path.

She froze in the kitchen doorway. “Oh. My. God.” I set my car-seat baby basket down and looked over her shoulder. The floor was covered in leftovers—some eaten, some licked, some regurgitated. “He didn’t close the refrigerator door,” we said in unison.

A trail led to the dogs, who were lying on the couch, too full or sick to feel remorse or any urge to get up. “WHAT’S THIS?” Lorene said in her very-bad-dog voice. Vita’s brow furrowed. Mister’s chin never left the armrest. “WHAT’S THIS?!” Aurora started to cry.

This? This is our life.

My Big Bucket List

- [x] marriage
- [x] career
- [x] house
- [x] baby

Postpartum Impressions

Life was what happened while we were busy coming up with our new routines. Balance was like a direction on a compass, a bearing we set ourselves on, not some specific place where we ever hoped to actually arrive.

AURORA'S MILESTONES

Aurora's birth certificate was recorded, registered, sealed, and delivered to our mailbox on December 3, 2004 —the same day she smiled for the first time. A couple months later, she rolled over. She was crawling by the end of the summer, speed-crawling during her first Ride FAR, and she had been walking for three months when we made our first family trip to Australia in February of 2006.

The Commonwealth of Massachusetts
DEPARTMENT OF PUBLIC HEALTH
REGISTRY OF VITAL RECORDS AND STATISTICS
STANDARD CERTIFICATE OF LIVE BIRTH

STATE USE ONLY
3D. REGISTERED NUMBER 19089

CHILD
3C. CITY/TOWN BOSTON
3B. COUNTY SUFFOLK
3A. FACILITY NAME-IF NOT IN FACILITY, NUMBER AND STREET BRIGHAM AND WOMEN'S HOSPITAL
NAME 4A. FIRST AURORA 4B. MIDDLE JEAN 4C. LAST BECKER
5. SEX FEMALE 6A. PLURALITY SINGLE 6B. BIRTH ORDER —
7. TIME 05:25 AM 8. DATE OF BIRTH (Month, Day, Year) OCTOBER 29,2004

MOTHER
NAME 10A. FIRST SUZANNE 10B. MIDDLE ROSE 10C. LAST BECKER 10D. MAIDEN SURNAME BECKER
BIRTHPLACE 11A. CITY/TOWN PHILADELPHIA 11B. STATE/COUNTRY PENNSYLVANIA
12. DATE OF BIRTH (Month, Day, Year) SEPTEMBER 24,1962
RESIDENCE 13A. NUMBER AND STREET SOUTH BOLTON RD 13B. CITY/TOWN BOLTON 13C. COUNTY WORCESTER 13D. STATE MA 13E. ZIP CODE 01740

NAME 14A. FIRST * LORENE 14C. LAST JEAN

INFORMANT
17A. I (WE) CERTIFY THAT THE PERSONAL INFORMATION APPEARING ABOVE IS TRUE AND CORRECT
17C. DATE SIGNED (Month, Day, Year) NOVEMBER 8,2004
17D. MAILING ADDRESS NUMBER AND STREET
17B. RELATIONSHIP TO CHILD PARENTS
18. DATE OF RECORD (Month, Day, Year) NOV 16 2004
19. SUPPLEMENT FILED (Month, Day, Year)
21. DPH USE ONLY * SECOND PARENT
20. CLERK/REGISTRAR

We're legally a family!

I streamlined my workload. I gave up environmental cartooning and focused on parenting, pet, and other cartoons and books, which I could draw from my day-to-day experience.

Lorene back-burnered her doula business. She didn't want to be running out on our baby in the middle of the night to help someone else have hers. She sold her house. And she rented an office above her shop so she could take Aurora to "work."

AURORA'S
OFFICE

JOURNAL: JULY 10, 2006

The past nineteen months have gone by faster than any I can remember. I think time used to go by more slowly when it seemed like the Future (when I'd have everything I ever wanted) would never get here.

Now that I no longer felt the need to plan for a lifetime, I made a plan for one day.

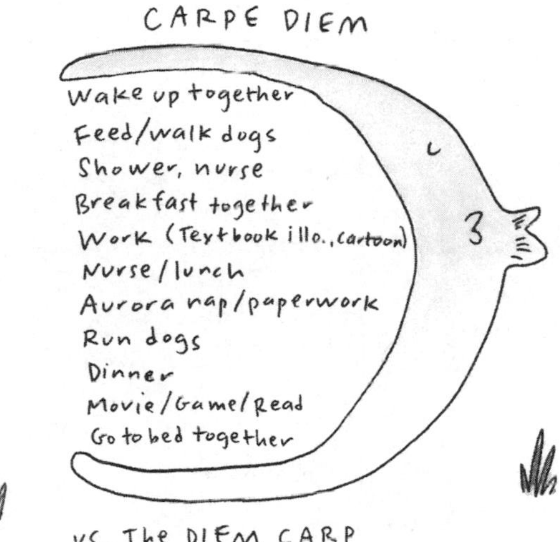

My neighbor Margaret is at the door. She is returning some eggs she borrowed. Not the one egg she borrowed the afternoon of my first retrieval—that was five years earlier. Aurora is three. We've stopped counting her age in months. I've stopped feeling like an imposter; the words "my daughter" roll right off my tongue.

"God, it's such a relief seeing your place looking like this. I can remember coming over here when my kids were young—I was so jealous. It looked like a museum!"

"Thanks, Margaret."

I can remember caring what people thought about the way my house looked. Trying to ban the plastic items at first, then keeping them

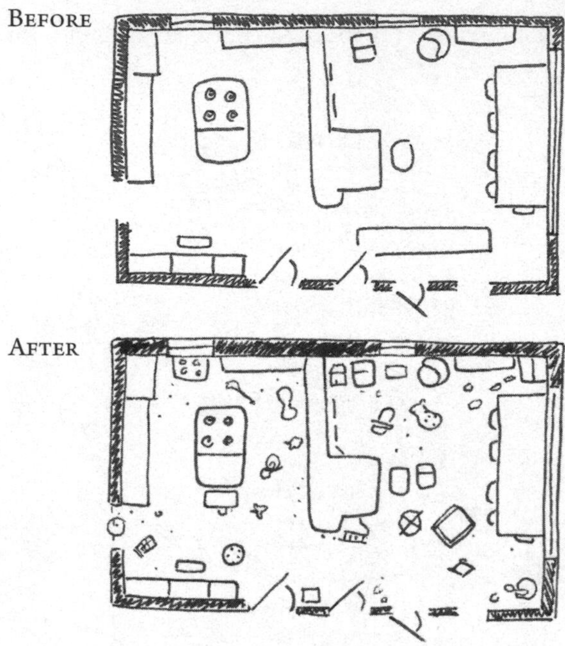

at bay, insisting on getting them back into the correct bins and boxes, then letting go. Not completely. I have to tell myself *The Velveteen House* story. Our house has been made Real.

There are so many things I didn't know to factor into the baby decision back when I was making it, like this connection to neighbors, strangers, other mothers everywhere. The fear of other people's disapproval has no basis in my reality. If anything, people have expressed a little envy of Lorene's and my shared parenting. We each have a wife.

"MAMA!" Aurora is calling. I am everything except Ma, that's Lorene. There has never been any confusion, save a few days when Bruce was Mommy Bruce and we had to clarify that "Mommy" is reserved for actual mothers, not just someone who does your bidding.

"Just a minute," I call back.

"I'll let you go," Margaret says, and lets herself out.

"Mommy, can you tell me the Laya burp story?"

"Sweetie, I can't tell you a Laya story while I'm cooking, I have to think." I've told her the story a hundred times and you would think I wouldn't have to think, but I have to tell it as if I'm Laya, the doll Daddy Steve gave her for her third birthday.

"Pinky Delicious!" Lorene bursts through the door and saves me.

After dinner, I get the dishes started and Lorene helps Aurora get ready for bed. The two of them call when it's time, and Lorene and I trade places. Aurora is lying in her big-girl bed, a toddler bed that sleeps one small person comfortably. She has the framed picture of Daddy Steve beside her pillow and she is inhaling an open Ziploc. "See, Laya? It smells just like Daddy." It's his T-shirt.

I fold myself in beside her. "Does it make you sad?" Laya asks.

1000 NAMES for BABY

Kimpy
Minky
Monkey
Peanut
Mrs. McGillicuddy
Cuckoo
Kookala
The A-Bomb
Pookie
Bub/Bud

"No. Some parents go away and never come back. It's like a business trip, Laya. Daddy always comes back," Aurora explains.

"Okay, what am I reading?" I ask her. She points to a big book of fairy tales. She wants to hear *The Little Mermaid*.

" . . . Looking through the porthole, she sees the prince. Her heart pounds. It was love at first sight."

"What is 'love at first sight'?" she asks.

Real ~~TRUE~~ LOVE

"When you fall in love before you even know somebody."

"Did that happen with you and Ma?"

"Ma and I knew each other for a long time before we fell in love. Love at first sight is more of a fairy tale thing."

"Oh. I want to be David."

"You wish you were a boy?" Aurora shakes her head no. "You wish you were older?"

"I wish Ma was twenty-eight when I was born. I forget, how old were you when you had me?"

"Forty-two. Sorry."

"Why forty-two?"

oh goodness, I'm pregnant AGAIN!

Ask Mary. "If I hadn't waited so long, I might have had someone else. Sarah Nastyman or Doshua Stump or . . . " I won't say it was all meant to be, the brain surgery and everything; but I will say I am so lucky it is. Now that they've favored me (with my old eggs and defective tube), I can acknowledge the incredible odds against all of it.

"Let's get back to the mermaid," I say. After the story ends, she falls fast asleep. I let the toddler-sleep vapors overtake me and wake up twenty minutes later. I fix the covers, smooth her hair, and whisper, "I love you . . . more than you love ice cream." Then I pad next door to change into my pajamas. Fresh from a power nap, I am ready to start the night shift in my studio.

Three hours later, I can see our bedroom light go out. An extra hush falls over the house.

It's even better than you dreamed.

acknowledgments

It took a village to write this book. A bottomless thank-you to my agent Edite Kroll who read and thoughtfully edited the manuscript more times than one would think humanly possible. Then again, I think she's superhuman. It was a privilege to work with my editor Nancy Miller and the rest of the Bloomsbury team: Lea Beresford, Laura Phillips, Sara Mercurio, Patti Ratchford, Cristina Gilbert, Laura Keefe, Alona Fryman, and Megan Ernst. I would also like to thank my village readers: Brooke James, Susan Oblak, Janet Zade, Bill Strong, Kathy McCullough, Robin Becker, and Marcy Krasnow. Their insights made this a much better book. I am heavily indebted to the all-night kind-but-ruthless editing services of Karen Dukess and Kathleen Cushman. And I am probably indentured to the book's designer, the talented and unflappable Cia Boynton.

Big thanks to Birdsong at Morning, Robin Becker, Tamara Grogan, Hilary Price, the Jameses, the Ewing-Hannans, the Nashes, and the Park Slope Community Bookstore for generously sharing their spaces, and to the Lachances, the Oblaks, the Rabinowitzes, the Carrolls, and the Rezacs for the play dates which made it possible for me to finish this book.

I'd also like to acknowledge a couple of divine interventions (friends I made in my advanced maternal age)—Brooke James and Nancy Aronie. And my dear old friend (a.k.a. Aurora's new best friend Big) Bruce Kohl, who is practically family. Which leaves my family itself—the Wicks-Beckers, Robin Becker, Alan Becker, Linda Mita, the Butmores, Steve Dillon, Lorene Jean, and Aurora Jean Becker—the people for whom I would do anything and who have done the same for me, over and over and over.

About Suzy Becker

Author, artist, educator, and entrepreneur Suzy Becker began her career as an award-winning advertising copywriter and then founded the Widget Factory, a greeting-card company. She entered the world of books with what would become the internationally best-selling *All I Need to Know I Learned from My Cat,* and has since written and illustrated several award-winning books for both children and adults. She and her family live in central Massachusetts.

Visit her website at www.suzybecker.com.